Seven Steps to Recruit-Proof Your Child

In Memory of Dennis "Sonny" Weaver

A friend who left the "gay" lifestyle too late
to escape the deadly grip of AIDS

Seven Steps to Recruit-Proof Your Child

A parent's guide to protecting children from
homosexuality and the "gay" movement.

By Scott Lively

Published by Founders Publishing Corporation
PO Box 20307
Keizer, Oregon 97307

Copyright 1998 by Lively Communications Inc.
PO Box 5271, Salem, Oregon 97304

First Edition 0123456789

ISBN 0-9647609-5-9

Table of Contents

Introduction.. ii

Step One: Get Serious... 1

Step Two: Take Authority... 23

Step Three: Inform Yourself... 47

Step Four: Strengthen Your Family................................... 83

Step Five: Improve Your Parenting Skills........................ 115

Step Six: Clean House.. 137

Step Seven: Be Active In Your Community..................... 159

Epilogue: What To Do When It's "Too Late".................. 197

Recommended Resources... 207

Appendix: Warning Signs... 209

Seven Steps to Recruit-Proof Your Child

ACKNOWLEDGMENTS

This book would not have been possible without the encouragement and assistance of many friends and associates. First on the list is the wonderful group of friends that make up our regular Saturday night discussion group in our home: Ron and Jan Galla-Rini, Bob and June Shelly (it was Bob who really got me started on this book with a conversation about "gay" recruitment), Simon and Emily Cassar, Charles and Kathy Lowers, Joy Kim and Dale Dieleman. Thanks for bearing with me through many hours of talk about this project and for all your good suggestions and feedback. Special thanks go to friends who provided materials which we used here. Lou and Beverly Sheldon of Traditional Values Coalition, Richard Sweeny, Arthur Delaney, Peter LaBarbera, Betty McConkey, Dr. Charles Socarides, Josh Handschuh, Mark Pertuit, Kevin E. Abrams, Alan Medinger, Anthony Falzarano, Laurette Elsberry and Tres Kerns. Thanks to Joy Kim and Noah Lively for typing assistance. Lastly, I would like to thank the many ex-"gay" leaders and workers who responded with such positive feedback when they learned of this project. Your encouragement made this job a lot easier.

AUTHOR'S NOTE

There are two types of readers in this world: those who like their reading material simple and to the point and those who want lots of documentation. This book attempts to accommodate both types. Our observations and advice to parents are provided in a straightforward, informal style on the right-hand pages. Our documentation and illustrations are provided on the left-hand pages, roughly parallel to the assertions they support. We believe that our readers will find this format helpful and "user friendly."

A Tough Approach for a Tough Subject

This book takes a "tough love" approach to homosexuality. Because we care about our "gay" friends and neighbors, we decline to affirm their unhappy and destructive lifestyle. We also care deeply about our children's health and happiness and for this reason we speak frankly and unapologetically in this book about homosexuality and the "gay" movement. Some will call this book hateful, but it is not motivated by hate, but by love, love that is tough enough to endure being misunderstood and maligned by the very people it seeks to help, love that rejects the easy path of condoning others' harmful choices simply to avoid personal discomfort.

The primary goal of this book is to help parents protect their children, but it will serve an even greater purpose if it also inspires in its readers an attitude of "tough love" that can help those already trapped in the "gay" lifestyle to escape.

Introduction

"Gay" by Choice or by Chance?

Who Gets the Benefit of the Doubt?

The title of this book is going to make some people unhappy. They will argue that you *can't* protect someone from homosexuality because homosexuals are "born that way" and have no choice in the matter. The fact is that science has *not* proved that homosexuality is biologically caused. A handful of scientific studies in the past few years have claimed to show a possible biological (genetic) cause of homosexuality, but these studies were conducted by "gay" activists themselves and have largely been rejected by non-"gay" scientists. The failure to demonstrate a genetic basis for homosexuality doesn't prove that homosexuals are *not* born that way, but then, it doesn't have to. The logical presumption of science must be that an unproved hypothesis is simply not true. Further, the burden of proof should always be with the proponent of a new idea, not the defender of the established view of things. As with so many "politically correct" issues, however, logic has been turned on its head as it relates to homosexuality and the "gay" political agenda. Advocates of homosexuality will, when forced, grudgingly acknowledge that science has not proved a biological cause for it, but they nevertheless insist their belief is true and that the burden of proof that homosexuality not innate should be on those who believe it is a learned behavior.

Unfortunately, many people have accepted this faulty logic and taken the position that we should give homosexuals the benefit of the doubt; we should treat them as if homosexuality were already proved to be a normal variant of human sexuality. After all, the reasoning goes, if homosexuals truly are "born that way," it would be unfair to treat them as if homosexuality were a simple lifestyle choice that they could change. No one has adequately explained how the discovery of a biological cause for homosexuality would legitimize homosexual behavior, but that is part of the assumption we are asked to accept. However, many human behaviors are influenced by biological factors, and not all of them are good for the individual or society.

Meanwhile, serious questions have gone unasked in America's rush to be "fair" to homosexuals. What if homosexuality is *not* biologically determined? (Again, the weight of evidence indicates that it is not.) What if homosexuality is a learned behavior, or worse, a type of sexual addiction that, once started, is very hard to stop? Who stands to be harmed by unchecked homosexual advocacy in our society? Aren't our children at the greatest risk? Leaving aside the question of whether "gays" recruit, what if some children choose to experiment with homosexuality simply because they are taught by teachers or role models that it is a normal sexual alternative? Many opponents of the "gay" movement believe that this is true and offer compelling evidence to support their position.

This book suggests that our society is giving the wrong people the benefit of the doubt on the question of homosexuality. Rather than assuming that science will eventually vindicate the belief that homosexuality is both normal and innate, we should be asking what harm might come to our children if homosexuality is a harmful, learned behavior. In our opinion, if there is *any* question about whether children can be protected from becoming homosexual we should act in a manner which will protect the children. Any other response allows our children to be used as guinea pigs in a dubious social experiment. In short, it is our children, and not "gay" political activists, who deserve the benefit of the doubt.

Some will suggest that such a policy implies that society should discriminate against homosexuals. If discrimination is defined as irrational or arbitrary prejudice, then certainly we should not discriminate. However, if discrimination means choosing between competing rights based on a legitimate priority (the health of our children), we *should* discriminate. We should not be afraid to say no to the "gay" political movement when its goals conflict with our policy of putting children first. All rights are balanced with responsibilities. Freedom of speech does not allow shouting "Fire!" in a crowded theater. Freedom of sexual preference should not allow teaching children that "gay" is good.

**IT'S TRUE...
WE *ARE*
RECRUITING.**

The Multnomah County Children & Youth Services Commission invites you to join us in one of several rewarding opportunities. The Commission has set a high priority on meeting the needs of girls & young women, racial & ethnic minority youth, and sexual minority youth. Gay men & Lesbians are welcome!
- Apply to become a Youth Commission member.
- Join one of several task forces or committees.
- Attend a work session to plan for media advocacy.
- Consider offering your financial support.

MULTNOMAH COUNTY OREGON

SOCIAL SERVICES DIVISION
YOUTH PROGRAM OFFICE
426 SW STARK STREET, 6TH FLOOR
PORTLAND, OREGON 97204

*Jim Clay
Program Development Specialist*
(503)

"Gay" activists flaunt their control of a government youth services agency in this ad from a "gay" publication. The headline mocks the notion of "gay" recruitment, yet exemplifies how recruitment of young people occurs.

"We finally realize that recruitment is the only answer...lesbian goals must be to recruit more lesbians."

Homosexual activist Kathy McDevitt, in an appearance before the Davis City, California City Council in 1980. *Davis Enterprise*, October 2, 1980.

"[I am] tired of the old chestnut that our movement for public acceptance has not increased and will not increase the number of gay men and lesbians in existence. 'There are more of us than there used to be.'"

Donna Minkowitz, "Recruit, Recruit, Recruit," *Advocate*, December 29, 1992.

Step One

Get Serious

Face the Truth — "Gays" Recruit

Every day in this country, hundreds of young people try out homosexual behavior for the very first time. In some cases, these experiments are with peers, but very often the sexual partner is an older person (sometimes much older) who has already identified himself or herself as "gay." Most of us think of recruitment as the seduction of an innocent, perhaps emotionally vulnerable child or youth by an older sexual predator. Consider, however, that even homosexual experimentation between peers can be evidence of "gay" recruitment. Recruitment is a mental and emotional process that begins long before the first sexual act occurs. In the truest sense of the word, "gay" recruitment is a process of changing someone's attitude about sexuality, rendering him or her more likely to take that first step into the "gay" lifestyle. In some cases, recruitment emboldens a person to initiate a homosexual contact, in others it simply makes the person more susceptible to being seduced.

In the relationship between recruitment and seduction we are not necessarily talking about pedophilia (adult/child sex), yet the process of "gay" recruitment is very similar to a tactic of pedophiles that psychologists call "grooming." In "grooming," an adult sexual

2

RECRUITMENT BEGINS WITH
MORAL REEDUCATION

"Anyone who embraces homosexuality in himself or herself as a joy to be celebrated is a gay person. Our work will only be finished when we can say that the whole world is gay."

From an editorial in a "gay" publication, "Making the Whole World Gay," cited in Charles Socarides, M.D., *Homosexuality, A Freedom Too Far*, p. 30, 1995.

"The campaign we outline...though complex, depends centrally upon a program of unabashed propaganda, firmly grounded in long-established principles of psychology and advertising."

"Gay" marketing gurus Marshall Kirk and Hunter Madsen, on their widely-followed blueprint for pro-"gay" social engineering. *After the Ball*, p. xxviii, 1990.

"At this point, getting the majority to say 'gay is good' at 9 or 10 years old is going to be difficult, but just because it is difficult doesn't mean its not the right thing."

Pepper Schwartz, University of Washington sociologist, speaking to a conference of educators and youth service providers, Beaverton, Oregon, April 23, 1992.

3

predator will sometimes spend years cultivating a relationship with a child, leading him or her into a sexual relationship only after the child has been thoroughly emotionally and mentally prepared. "Gay" recruitment is like "grooming," but it doesn't only occur on a one-to-one basis. The most insidious "gay" recruitment is being conducted by "gay" propagandists as a nationwide marketing and public relations campaign. In this campaign, all of our children are being "groomed" at the same time: their attitudes about homosexuality are being changed by one-sided, pro-"gay" propaganda in public education, in television programming, in movies, in music, in advertising, and in every other attitude-shaping institution influenced by "gay" activists.

Understanding this simple truth greatly increases our chances of protecting our children from homosexuality. Recruitment begins in the mind and in the emotions; it begins when a person is persuaded to consider trying homosexual behavior. Not every young person who concludes that "gay" is normal will experiment with homosexuality. Neither will every child who experiments become exclusively "gay." Yet we know that all children explore life's possibilities. When homosexuality is presented as a normal option (instead of being discouraged), many will experiment with it who otherwise wouldn't. Some of those will choose to stay in the "gay" lifestyle, or remain trapped there by this strongly addictive sexual behavior.

Social Conditioning Then and Now

Let's face it — much of what we believe and value is what we have been conditioned to believe and value. That's not necessarily wrong, provided that the things we believe are true, and the values we hold are good. As we grow older, most of us test our beliefs and values and, if need be, adjust them, having learned what is true and good. What is important to consider here is that conditioning plays a major part in shaping our attitudes, and that it works just as well in instilling false beliefs and bad values when these have become popular. Most of us were conditioned, as part of the training our

4

WHO CAN BE RECRUITED?

"The early teen years are a critical period when even a potentially 'straight' youngster could be encouraged to try gay sex, and could well establish an addiction to dangerous behavioral patterns."

Dr. Joseph Nicolosi, Executive Director of the National Association for the Research and Therapy of Homosexuality (NARTH), NARTH Bulletin, August, 1997.

"['Obligatory' homosexuals] are in the grip of unconscious forces and early life traumas over which they have no control. ['Optional' homosexuals] do have control; they get into same-sex because they like it. *Both types, however, can be seduced into same-sex sex.* According to one study of homosexual men done in 1990, some 37 percent of them were seduced into same-sex sex at an early age, by an uncle, or someone much older. Or, in the case of lesbians, seduced by an older woman."

Dr. Charles Socarides M.D. *Homosexuality, A Freedom Too Far*, pp. 18-19, 1995. (Emphasis ours.)

parents gave us, to reject sexual deviance. We learned our attitudes in many ways, and these attitudes were generally reinforced by society, even after the "sexual revolution" of the 1960s.

Partly because of this conditioning, most of us would not have seriously considered experimenting with homosexual behavior. However, we must not blindly assume that our children are being conditioned to our beliefs and values about sexuality. Children today are growing up in a far different social environment. Many of the moral values we take for granted are virtually absent from their world. When we left for school in the morning, our parents were justifiably confident that the educational system and the larger society would serve to reinforce their basic beliefs and values regarding sexuality. Today, that's just not true. Teachers are as likely as not to be socially liberal activists, possibly even "gay" activists. It has also become quite apparent that the style-setters of the popular culture and the media are very pro-"gay." If anything, today's educational system and its larger societal context are working *against* parents and not with them.

Just because you wouldn't have experimented with homosexuality, it doesn't follow that your child won't. On the other hand, if you did experiment with homosexuality and stopped because you were ashamed or were otherwise deterred by fear of social disapproval, consider what might have happened to you if you had conducted such an experiment in today's "gay-affirming" climate.

All Children Are Vulnerable to Recruitment

We mentioned in the introduction that "gay" science has not established that homosexuals are "born that way." Let us assume, for the sake of argument, that a biological cause for homosexuality *could* be found. If so, it would only apply to some, and not to all homosexuals. We know this because many "gays" openly reject the notion that they were born "gay," proudly and defiantly affirming their conscious preference for homosexuality. Many ex-"gays" admit that the "born that way" argument was, for them, nothing

Great achievers have been gay

Ann Landers

Dear Ann Landers: For the past few months, I have been thinking seriously about killing myself. I have tried to think of reasons not to, and the only one I can come up with is that it would cause my family a lot of grief.

I am 15 and feel so alone. I am scared. I feel worthless. The problem is I am absolutely certain that I am gay. At 15, a guy should be thinking about what he wants to do in life, not how to kill himself. I have always wanted to get married and have children, but I now know that lifelong dream is impossible. If there were some pill I could take to make all these sexual desires go away, I would gladly take it.

This isn't the easiest letter to write, Ann. I have nobody to talk to, and I need your advice more than anything. I can't talk to my mother because I am scared to death of how she would take it. Please, Ann, help me. I can't go on this way much longer. – Hampton, Va.

Dear Hampton: You are not alone. According to some studies, an estimated 10 percent of individuals, worldwide, are homosexual. Did you know that Alexander the Great, Leonardo DaVinci, Michelangelo, actor Rock Hudson, rock star Freddie Mercury, author Truman Capote, poet Allen Ginsberg and playwright Tennessee Williams were gay? They were outstanding in their fields and contributed a great deal to the world. Homosexuals are born, not made.

that I reprint the piece you sent. Many thanks. Here it is:

The difference between Winners and Whiners is –

The Whiner says, "I don't know, and I'm sure nobody else knows, either."

The Winner says, "Let's find out."

When a Whiner makes a mistake, he says, "It wasn't my fault."

When Bob Shelly of Chino Hills, California responded to this Ann Landers column on behalf of a young relative, he was referred to several pro-"gay" resources for kids, including Alyson Publications. Among other offensive products, Alyson Publications distributes this "gay" sex manual which offers the following advice for pederasts:

GAY SEX

A MANUAL FOR MEN WHO LOVE MEN

by JACK HART ♥ illustrated by BRADLEY M. LOOK

"Precautions: For men who are involved with partners under the legal age of consent, a member of NAMBLA (the North American Man/Boy Love Association) offers some suggestions to minimize the risk:...Don't...share information about your relationship...with anyone....Don't take photos of him....Such photos simply provide fuel for police and ambitious D.A.s....Don't record your experiences...Avoid situations where a number of men have sex with the same boy, or group of boys, over a period of time..."

Gay Sex: A Manual for Men Who Love

more than a convenient lie. Even the most dyed-in-the-wool "gay" activist, therefore, must acknowledge that at least some homosexuals are not "born that way."

As to the issue of whether recruitment is possible, then, we can say that some children (those who may have some predisposition toward homosexuality) are more vulnerable than others, but that one does not have to be "born that way" to become "gay." In other words, even if your child is not biologically predisposed to homosexuality, he or she could be recruited into the "gay" lifestyle under the right circumstances. This book will help you to avoid those circumstances.

Recruitment Also Occurs Through Non-"Gay" Homosexualists

Not all champions of the "gay" movement are homosexuals. For various reasons, many non-"gay" people are active in the cause of legitimizing homosexuality to children. (We use the word, homosexualist to refer to anyone, homosexual or not, who works to legitimize homosexuality in our society. Many non-homosexuals are homosexualists. Conversely, many nonpolitical homosexuals are *not* homosexualists). Often non-"gay" homosexualists are more effective than "gay" activists in promoting homosexuality to young people because they appear to be impartial observers not affected by "gay" self-interest. It is likely that many homosexualists are actually "in the closet" homosexuals (a great many active homosexuals, even political proponents of homosexuality, are not open about their involvement in the "gay" lifestyle). Many others are relatives or friends of "gay" activists who have been emotionally coerced or otherwise persuaded to the "gay" viewpoint. Whatever their motive, non-"gay" homosexualists play a big part in recruiting children into homosexuality, even though they themselves are not homosexual. (When in doubt about whether advocates of the "gay" agenda are homosexual or not, it is advisable to use the term "homosexualist" to avoid possible legal problems — it is ironic that many aggressive non-homosexual defenders of the "gay" lifestyle

GENERAL COLIN POWELL REJECTS "GAY"/RACE COMPARISON

General Colin Powell, first African-America to serve as Chairman of the U.S. Joint Chiefs of Staff.

"Skin color is a benign, non-behavioral characteristic. Sexual orientation is perhaps the most profound of all human behavioral characteristics. Comparison of the two is a convenient but invalid argument."

Letter to Congresswoman Pat Schroeder as quoted in the Salem Statesman-Journal, June 6, 1992.

"A parent confused over what is sexually appropriate is hardly able to provide helpful sexual guidance for a child. Influenced by various movements which stress doing your own thing as long as it is pleasurable, and, aware that the carefully structured society they grew up with is rapidly being chipped away, parents often feel helpless and cannot instill sexual values in their young because they themselves are so unsure of the boundaries."

Clifford L. Linedecker, *Children in Chains*, p. 118, 1981.

consider the suggestion that they themselves are "gay" to be defamatory.)

You May Unwittingly Be Helping the "Gay" Movement Recruit Your Child.

If "gay" recruitment begins with a change of attitude about sexuality, any endorsement that you as a parent give to "gay" propaganda claims will make your child more vulnerable to the total recruitment strategy. For example, the "gay" movement compares homosexuals to ethnic minorities in order to create the idea in people's minds that disapproval of homosexuality is just like racism. (Many parents have accepted this comparison without really thinking about it.) Since racism is (thankfully) almost universally condemned in America today, the person who accepts the "gay" racism association will probably also condemn disapproval of homosexuality. Obviously, someone who condemns disapproval of homosexuality is going to be both suspicious of arguments against "gay" behavior and susceptible to arguments in favor of it. Though the child may originally have no desire for or interest in homosexual behavior, once having begun to actively defend homosexuality, he or she will most certainly attract practicing "gays." At the same time, the "gay"-positive child or youth will contribute to shifting the attitudes of those in his or her entire peer group toward a pro- "gay" position. The more closely that a young person begins to identify with the "suffering" or "disadvantaged status" of "gays," the more vulnerable he or she will be to seduction.

Equally damaging is the harm which such thinking does to a child's ability to reason. It is self evident that homosexuality, even if caused by a genetic defect, is a form of behavior. Not only is it a form of behavior, but it is behavior with potentially life-threatening consequences. Being Black or Asian or Hispanic is completely behavior-neutral. To equate discrimination against harmful behavior with discrimination based on skin color is an affront to logic. A child who is taught to accept such illogic will be accepting of other faulty analogies and deceptive arguments.

RECRUITMENT STRATEGIES MANIPULATE PARENTS AND OTHER ROLE MODELS

"Give protectors a just cause. A media campaign that casts gays as society's victims and encourages straights to be their protectors must make it easier for those who respond to assert and explain their new protectiveness. Few straight women, and even fewer straight men, will want to defend homosexuality boldly as such....Our campaign should not demand direct support for homo*sexual* practices, but should instead take *anti-discrimination* as its theme. The right to free speech, freedom of beliefs, freedom of association, due process and equal protection of laws -- these should be the concerns brought to mind by our campaign."

Marshall Kirk and Erastus Pill, "The Overhauling of Straight America," *Guide Magazine*, November, 1987.

"We immediately seized upon the opponents' calling card -- safety -- and explained how homophobia represents a threat to students' safety by creating a climate where violence, name-calling, health problems and suicide are common....We knew that, confronted with real-life stories of youth who had suffered from homophobia, our opponents would automatically be put on the defensive; they would have to attack people who had been victimized once, which put them in a bully position from which it would be hard to emerge looking good."

Kevin Jennings, Gay, Lesbian and Straight Teachers Network (GLSEN), from a speech quoted in public testimony to Congress, July 2, 1996 by Peter LaBarbera.

"Gays" *are* like minorities in certain limited ways, such as being a distinct group of people and having suffered ill-treatment. But there are many extenuating circumstances even in the similarities: for example, that, despite having no identifying characteristics, they identify *themselves* as a group, and that ill-treatment has very often come from open or covert members of their own group. There are also many obvious and irreconcilable dissimilarities, such as that homosexuals as a group enjoy wealth and high levels of education and employment, and that they can and do voluntarily leave membership in the homosexual group (in contrast, there are no ex-Blacks or ex-Hispanics). We will distinguish between "gays" and minorities more thoroughly later, but here we only seek to demonstrate that parents' acceptance of "gay" propaganda claims weakens their children's emotional and intellectual defenses. Any position taken by parents on "gay" issues that fails to acknowledge that homosexuality is wrong and harmful hurts children by making them more susceptible to "gay" recruitment.

Use Moderation in Teaching
Disapproval of Homosexuality

Nothing in the above sections is intended to suggest to parents that they should teach their children to hate homosexuals. Indeed, we must be very careful *not* to promote hostility to homosexuals as people, both for their sakes and for our children's. Our hostility, if we have any, should be directed at the "gay" *movement* and its destructive agenda. The more abusively some people treat homosexual *individuals*, the more likely they are to offend children's natural sense of justice and fairness and cause them to rush to the defense of homosexual victims. (The "gay" movement knows of this tendency in children — and adults — and exploits it to the fullest, even to the point of fabricating evidence.) Parents must keep two things in mind about this aspect of the issue. First, one can have sympathy for homosexuals, treating them in a way which protects their dignity without condoning their behavior. Any child with basic reasoning skills can understand this distinction. Second,

EXCERPTS FROM <u>BOWERS V. HARDWICK</u>, THE 1986 SUPREME COURT CASE WHICH DEFINES THE *CURRENT* CONSTITUTIONAL STATUS OF LAWS AGAINST HOMOSEXUAL BEHAVIOR

"Respondent would have us announce...a fundamental right to engage in homosexual sodomy. This we are quite unwilling to do....Proscriptions against this conduct have ancient roots....Against this background, to claim that a right to engage in such conduct is 'deeply rooted in this Nation's history and tradition' or 'implicit in the concept of ordered liberty' is, at best, facetious."

Justice Byron White, writing for the majority. Bowers v. Hardwick, 478 U.S. 186, 106 S.Ct. 2841 (emphasis ours).

"I join the court's opinion, but I write separately to underscore my view that *in constitutional terms there is no such thing as a fundamental right to commit homosexual sodomy*....Decisions of individuals relating to homosexual conduct have been subject to state intervention throughout the history of Western civilization....Homosexual sodomy was a capital crime under Roman law....Blackstone described 'the infamous crime against nature' as an offense of 'deeper malignity' than rape, a heinous act 'the very mention of which is a disgrace to human nature...'"

Chief Justice Warren Berger, concurring opinion, Bowers v. Hardwick, 478 U.S. 186, 106 S.Ct. 2841 (emphasis ours).

even in situations where an individual has been inexcusably hatefully treated because of his homosexuality, his status of being a "victim" does not legitimize his homosexual behavior. We can compare this to the situation of a shoplifter caught red-handed and then severely beaten by a store security guard. The shoplifter is clearly a victim of unnecessary brutality, but no one would ever suggest that his crime should therefore be treated as normal and acceptable behavior by society.

Don't Fall Prey to the "Sexual Orientation" Trap

Your greatest enemy in the fight to protect your child from homosexuality is the theory of "sexual orientation." Sexual orientation became the central marketing theme of "gay" public relations following the 1986 Supreme Court case of Bowers v. Hardwick. In Bowers, the court forcefully rejected the idea that homosexual sodomy deserves civil rights protection under the right to privacy and upheld the right of States to criminalize homosexual acts. The right-to-privacy argument, which had been used since the rise of the American "gay" movement in the 1940s, acknowledged that homosexuality was defined by *behavior*. After this argument was finally lost in Bowers, the powerful "gay" movement began promoting the view that homosexuality is not behavior but a form of identity. In this new theory, homosexuality was said to have little to do with the sexual act, and everything to do with a person's natural sexual "orientation" toward persons of the same gender. Thus, a person could be "gay" even if he or she never had a single sexual encounter. Moreover, since orientation is supposedly something deeply personal and rooted in a person's self-awareness, no one but the "gay" person can ever know whether he or she is homosexual. In one deceptive stroke, the "gay" movement turned public attention from what homosexuals *do* to what homosexuals supposedly *are*, making themselves the only ones who could define that identity.

14

RECRUITMENT BY DECEIT

"Teenagers are specifically encouraged to *use only their feelings* as a guide to sexual behavior; to be their own judge of right and wrong; and to 'have fun' experimenting. If a sexual behavior feels good, the logic says, it will tell them 'who they are.' Teenagers are encouraged to see religious traditionalists as mean-spirited, while at the same time to see gay consciousness as 'sacred.'"

Dr. Joseph Nicolosi, discussing literature and books for children which are recommended by Parents and Friends of Lesbians and Gays (P-FLAG). "A Closer Look at P-Flag," *Narth Bulletin*, April 1998.

"At age twelve, 25.9% of the children were 'unsure' of their sexual orientation."

Alan P. Medinger, "Adolescents and Homosexuality - Close Look at a Major Study," pp. 1-2, *Regeneration News*, February, 1993. Study of 34,000 children.

"Homosexuality and heterosexuality can neither be prevented nor created. They simply are, to be discovered from within, or to emerge as one's life progresses....Sexual orientation is immutable and recruitment in either direction is impossible."

Frank Kameny, "'Ex-Gay' zealots should heed the golden rule," *THE WASHINGTON BLADE*, March 21, 1997.

How Sexual Orientation Theory Threatens Your Child

Sexual orientation theory implies (contrary to the available evidence) that children who experiment with homosexuality or express homosexual feelings are "born that way." More importantly, it also implies that all other children are born with a heterosexual orientation and that neither homosexual nor heterosexual persons can change their orientation. Parents who have accepted the concept of sexual orientation (and those who haven't may be the exception) are thus lulled into believing that their "heterosexually oriented" children are safe from "gay" recruitment or homosexual experimentation. Our own parents would never have put up with "gay" activists coming into the schools to talk about their lifestyle with children, but many parents today just aren't concerned. They think they are helping their children to be tolerant of people who are simply different by an accident of birth. They don't think it is possible that *their* child could become "gay." But when a "gay" activist tells a classroom of middle-schoolers that, statistically speaking, ten percent of them are probably "gay," every one of those children immediately wonders if he or she might be among the ten percent (homosexuals actually account for less than two percent of the population). Most of them probably dismiss the idea eventually, but how many do not? Imagine being a 12-year-old boy who has been the target of playground bullies' taunts of "sissy" or "fag." Suppose the boy has recently been rejected by a girl he likes. Will he so quickly dismiss the question? Imagine a physically unattractive young girl who has been mocked and ridiculed by the same crowd of bullies and found solace in a deep friendship with another girl. Will she confuse her love of her friend with homosexual "orientation?"

The Ultimate Recruitment Tool

Sexual orientation theory is the ultimate recruitment tool of the "gay" movement. Since the supposed orientation is only discovered through self-awareness, anything that can influence self-awareness can influence orientation. Self-awareness is largely a process of

MONDAY, APRIL 6, 1998

As gay teachers come out, so does controversy

SOC...
sm...
vea...
som...
tellin...

By MAR...
The Asso...

SAN
San F...
them. I
worlds
One,
ence t...
came o...
dents o...
ance la...
a flurr...
"Is tl...
insecur...
lems,
James
a lette...
school district fire ner.

"You can find gay, lesbian and bisexual staff and students at every school level from kindergarten through high school ...And every day, their numbers grow.... gay and lesbian issues are no longer addressed only in the most diverse city high schools or the most progressive private schools; they've burst out of the closet and spilled onto the table in virtually every school in the country. There's no turning back."

Doug Woog, *School's Out*, p. 133-135, 1995.

sex-
chil-
r of
ing
tell-
sim-
ves
art-
who
the
San
who
con-
she
job.
ll, a
nish
the
only
ach-

s to
t be
myself. It just ate away at me,"

17

searching and experiencing our emotions. Now, nothing is more easily manipulated in human beings than the emotions, and the most emotionally malleable human beings of all are children. Remember that sexual orientation theory doesn't define homosexuality by whether one engages in homosexual acts, but by whether one has homosexual feelings toward someone of the same gender. The average child with strong feelings of love or affection towards a same-sex friend or adult role model is vulnerable (especially during adolescence) to mistaking those normal and healthy feelings for an innate homosexual "orientation." If this is true for the average child, imagine how much greater the tendency if the child has a family with serious problems, or an alcoholic parent, or a history of rejection by peers, or a traumatic memory of having been sexually molested, or any other life complication that renders his or her emotions volatile and confused.

Now imagine that *you* are a young person with deep-seated gender identity confusion which began in early childhood. Perhaps you failed to bond with your parent of the same sex at that critical point in infancy when many psychotherapists believe gender identity is formed. Or maybe you just happened to get too much of the wrong biological "stuff" that characterizes maleness or femaleness (body size and shape, voice, hormonal make-up). For you, sexual orientation theory has created an almost unavoidable trap. You don't even have to have a homosexual encounter to be assumed by others to be "gay." And although you might otherwise have a very good chance to overcome the obstacles of your birth and background and enjoy a normal sexual life, the presumption that you are "born that way" may prevent anyone, even your own family, from ever trying to help you.

Wake Up to "Gay" Recruitment in the Schools

As a parent, you should know that pro- "gay" presentations are becoming very commonplace in public schools. (A book called *School's Out* brags that homosexual teachers may be found in every school in America.) These instructional sessions are not confined to

PRO-"GAY" TEACHING STRATEGIES

"These teaching strategies were provided by the school district to its teachers during "gay" sensitvity training at Grant High School:

1. Address negative school-based incidents on the spot — targeted harassment, put-downs (whether or not targeted to individuals), anti-gay jokes and grafitti, and labeling.

2. *Change language that assumes everyone is or should be heterosexual (use "partner" rather than boyfriend or girlfriend, "permanent relationship" rather than marriage).*

3. Change human relations and personnel policies to protect students and staff from discrimination on the basis of sexual orientation; train personnel to follow up violations.

4. Identify gay/lesbian contributions throughout the curriculum (history, literature, art, science, religion, etc.).

5. Provide history of oppression (such as the Holocaust, origins of defamatory terms for gay people).

6. Submit requests to improve library holdings (both fiction and nonfiction) related to sexual diversity.

7. Develop and/or advertise resources (support groups) for lesbian/gay students and their families.

8. Include issues for gay/lesbian students and staff in coverage in school newspaper.

9. *Bring in openly gay/lesbian adults as resources in classes and assemblies.*

10. Include gay/lesbian concerns in all prevention programs (suicide, dropout, pregnancy, etc.) and in training of peer leaders, student government, etc.

Portland *Oregonian*. Sunday, February 25, 1996. (Emphasis ours.)

high school or junior high. A training video called "It's Elementary" teaches elementary school teachers how to get the "gay" message into primary grade classrooms. More subtle methods are used with preschoolers. Books like *Daddy's Roommate* and *Heather Has Two Mommies* ostensibly teach children about "alternative" families, and are objectionable on that basis alone — but the real purpose of such books is to introduce young children to the idea that "gay" is good. How much easier will it be for an adult predator to seduce these children in later years after they have been conditioned, virtually from infancy, to accept homosexuality?

Are these "gay" recruitment activities being carried out covertly by a few renegade homosexualist teachers? Certainly not. There are actual guidelines for promoting homosexuality in public schools which have been openly adopted by the National Education Association, the largest teacher's union in America.

Don't Be Complacent

When a child voices personal questions about the possibility of being "gay" to school officials, the parents may never hear about it. The child is often referred to outside "gay" counseling centers run by active homosexuals. Such "gay" centers are the equivalent of military recruiting offices whose purpose is to draw young people into the gay lifestyle. These centers often distribute literature filled with graphic sexual imagery, including drawings and photographs of men engaged in oral and anal sodomy and of more bizarre perversions with names like "rimming" and "fisting." If you think this kind of thing is a rarity in homosexual literature, pick up any "gay" newspaper or magazine and thumb through it. (If you don't know where to find one, check your local big-city library or community center — these publications will often be very prominent among the stacks of free newspapers, and are usually very accessible to children.)

Often the first time parents hear about a child's gender identity problem is when the child or young person confesses it to them or "comes out." This, of course, usually occurs long after the "gay"

RECRUITMENT BY
HOMOSEXUALIST EDUCATORS

"Teachers who practice homosexual acts are between 90 to 100 times more likely to involve themselves sexually with pupils than teachers who confine themselves to heterosexual acts."

Dr. Paul Cameron, "Homosexual Molestation of Children," *Psychological Reports*, vol. 57, p. 1227, 1985.

"In schools all over the country, children ...are being labeled 'sexual minority' students and are being led to counselors drawn almost exclusively from the gay community. How often are the deeply rooted needs and biases of these 'counselors' going to lead them to counsel the 'unsure' that they are gay? 'Unsure' in their minds often means that the youngster is simply afraid of coming to terms with his or her homosexuality ....Regeneration is a healing ministry, and we generally avoid the purely political side of homosexuality. However, what is going on in some school systems is more than political; our children's lives are being sacrificed to appease a minority and to further a political cause."

Alan Medinger, "Adolescents and Homosexuality - Close Look at a Major Study," pp. 1-2. *Regeneration News*. February, 1993.

identity has solidified in the young person's mind. For many people, once this has occurred, it is too late. Once a person has been drawn in by the cult-like seductiveness of the "gay" lifestyle, with its many reinforcements, he or she is statistically likely to remain in that lifestyle — despite all of the misery that attends it. This is why parents must act *before* their child is recruited. You must act *now* to protect your child from homosexuality

Gays applaud as court OKs adoptions by parent's partner

FAMILIES: A split pan-
el says couples — h
erosexual or gay —
must be extended th
same parental privi-
leges as single adult

By JOEL STASHENKO
The Associated Press

ALBANY, N.Y. — In a
hailed by gay-rights advoc
New York's highest cour
clared Thursday that unma
people — gay or heterosex
have a right to adopt their
ners' children.

Since state laws recogniz
relationships, the Court o
peals decided in a 4-3 vote

"To rule otherwise
mean that the thousands o
York children actually
raised in homes headed b

dith Kaye wrote.

Yorkers for Constitutional Free-

Homosexuality not illness, psychologists reaffirm

MENTAL HEALTH: The American Psychological Association calls on therapists to help re- move any stigma asso- ciated with being gay.

The Associated Press

CHICAGO — Homosexuality is not a mental disorder and doesn't need treatment, the na- tion's largest group of psycholo- gists has declared in an attempt to quell controversy over so- called reparative therapy.

The American Psychological Association, by a vote of its na- tional policy-setting board Thurs- day, also called on mental health professionals to "take the lead in removing the stigma of mental illness that has long been associ- ated with homosexual orienta- tion."

The association first declared in 1975 that homosexuality was not a mental disorder, as it sup- ported the American Psychiatric Association in removing it from

the official list of mental and emotional disorders.

The newest resolution said lack of information, ignorance and prejudice puts some "gay, lesbian, bisexual and questioning individuals at risk" for seeking "conversion" or "reparative" therapy, which is aimed at re- ducing or eliminating homosex- uality.

There have been no well-de- signed scientific studies to test such therapy, the association said in a statement.

But it has it been controver- sial enough to persuade that such therapy feeds upon soci- ety's anti-gay prejudices and is likely to exacerbate the client's sense of poor self-esteem, the association's officer said.

Kim Mills, a representative of the Human Rights Campaign, a lesbian and gay political group, said the resolution "reaffirms the fact that being there is noth- ing wrong with homosexuality, there is no reason that gay, lesbi- an or bisexual people should try to change."

"Robert H. Knight, director of

The newest
resolution said
lack of
information,
ignorance and
prejudice puts
some 'gay,
lesbian, bisexual
and questioning
individuals at
risk.'

cultural studies for the conserva- tive Family Research Council, said "homosexual behavior en- tail unstable physical and psy- chological risks" and main- tained that homosexuals have been successfully treated for bor disorder.

"Homosexuals can change," he said.

Be a Big Brother.

Leaders throughout our society have succumbed to "gay" political pressure. You are your child's last line of defense!

"Parents have the original, primary, and inalienable right to educate their children, and it is the place of schools to assist them. But rights not asserted are rights lost by default. Parental rights are not self-enforcing; they have to be exercised by vigilant and concerned parents."

Arthur J. Delaney, "The Grotesque World of Today's Sex Education," *New Oxford Review*, p. 16, May 1996.

Step Two

Take Authority

You Have the Right to Protect Your Child from Homosexuality.

If your initial response to the above statement is "Of course I have the right to protect my child from homosexuality!" your child is probably in pretty good hands. If, on the other hand, you are a parent who feels you must defer to "experts" to find answers to difficult child-rearing questions, this chapter is essential reading. Powerful forces are at work in our society to change your child's attitude about homosexuality and very few dissenting voices are able to make themselves heard. You may be the only important role model your child ever hears making a case against homosexual behavior and the "gay" lifestyle. You must be informed about the issue, certainly, but even more importantly, you must have confidence in your moral authority to contradict the "politically correct" propaganda of the "gay" movement. It is not as easy as you might think. This chapter will help you to affirm and to assert your parental authority in the face of those who would usurp it.

DENYING PARENTS' AUTHORITY

"The Judeo-Christian prejudice against homosexuality is arbitrary, absurd and evil."

Marshall Kirk and Hunter Madsen, *After the Ball*, p. 290, 1990.

"Homosexual sex is not only not immoral, sinful, wrong, or undesirable, but is affirmatively moral, virtuous, right, and desirable, and as much so as heterosexual sex. Adopting their terms, we must make it clear that homosexuality is a God-given blessing, to be enjoyed to its fullest. All of this must be put forward as a moral absolute, as absolute as their 'moral absolutes.'"

Frank Kameny, "'Ex-Gay' zealots should heed the golden rule," *The Washington Blade*, March 21, 1997.

"'We think gay teens should be supported in coming out,' was how Ms. Kane of the National Gay and Lesbian Task Force put it to me. But come out with whom? Clearly not their fellow 15-year-olds, who are presumably just as confused on the issue as they are. No, the guidance and the sex, tends to come from adult gays who bring the teens out. A study published in the *Journal of Pediatrics* showed that of a sample of gay teenagers who had steady sexual partners, the mean age of the partners was 25 years."

Paul Mulshine, *Heterodoxy*, September 1994.

The "Gay" Movement Claims You Do Not Have This Right

The "gay" myth of sexual orientation claims that some children are "gay" by birth and cannot change. Therefore, its proponents say, "gay" children should be affirmed in their homosexual identity and should not be forced into an "unnatural" heterosexual lifestyle. As the reasoning goes, parental and societal efforts to impose heterosexual norms on "gay" children are cruel and harmful, leading to serious mental and emotional problems. It is the supposedly unenlightened and bigoted attitude behind these efforts which causes "gay" youth suicides and drug and alcohol addiction.

There are a couple of problems with this reasoning. First, the conclusion that mere disapproval of homosexuality *causes* "gay" suicides is a classic *post hoc* fallacy. (In formal logic, a *post hoc* fallacy is the attribution of a false cause to an effect: either mistaking what is not the cause of a given effect to be the cause, or inferring that because one circumstance follows another in time it must be caused by the earlier circumstance.) There is absolutely no proof that the emotional problems of active homosexuals arise exclusively or even mostly from the disapproval of parents and society. Second, conspicuously absent from the public discussion of the "gay" youth issue is the question of whether suicidal and homosexual thoughts are *each* symptoms of yet deeper emotional problems.

Ignoring this possibility appears grossly negligent considering the fact that if, as many doctors believe, homosexuality is itself an indicator of deeper emotional problems, affirming children in their supposed "gayness" actually puts them at far greater risk than discouraging them. This risk is compounded by the presence of *many* other known health dangers (not only AIDS) faced by practicing homosexuals. Additionally, the "solutions" offered by "gay" activists to the problem of at-risk "gay" youth are blatantly self-serving and raise serious questions about their motivations. Such solutions include demands for direct access to schoolchildren to educate them about the "gay" identity and for referrals of questioning children to unsupervised homosexual-staffed "counseling" centers.

"SAFE SCHOOLS"

"Efforts to affirm so-called homosexual youth advance under the rubric of promoting 'diversity' and enhancing 'self-esteem' -- two fads in today's faltering public schools. The campaign rests on several tendentious suppositions that have barely begun to be fully debated by the larger society, foremost among them is the myth that a certain percentage of kids have a 'gay' (or lesbian, bisexual or transgendered) 'identity' which they are likely born with, and which is unchangeable. Educators are tasked with affirming such children and helping them cope in the midst of a homophobic culture. With this goal in mind of shoring up the 'gay minority' of students, gay activists have chosen a strategy of promoting, not homosexuality, but 'safe schools.' The cunning strategy relies heavily on winning public sympathy for 'gay youth' as a besieged victim group."

"One lesbian teacher recently made headlines by using a pink triangle to inform students that her class was a 'safe zone' for 'gays.'"

Peter LaBarbera, Testimony to Congress regarding the Defense of Marriage Act (DOMA), July 2, 1996.

"Gay" Activists Claim a Moral High Ground They Don't Deserve

In taking the position that "gay" youths are endangered by those who decline to affirm their self-identification as homosexuals, "gay" activists not only justify their own sexual activities, but also attempt to turn the tables on the rest of society. By pretending to hold the moral high ground, the "gay" movement puts parents on the defensive, portraying them as selfish and ignorant for wanting their children to have a normal heterosexual life. Unfortunately, this notion has served as a very effective argument for getting "gay" activists into the schools to "find" and to "help" homosexual youths.

Under the presumptions of sexual orientation theory, a parent's only defense against the charge of wrongfully suppressing a child's "gay" identity is to claim that the child is not "gay." As we have seen, this is generally a losing proposition, since defining someone as "gay" is, according to this theory, totally within the control of the person himself. Unfortunately, by the time the possibility is openly discussed, the child has often come under the influence of the local "gay" community, which works with impressive efficiency to assimilate and retain its members.

Don't Be Intimidated by "Political Correctness."

Although its defenders will never admit it, "political correctness" is nothing more than a set of moral conclusions about social issues, which, its proponents insist, should be binding on all of us. Ironically, the other moral system which makes this claim of being binding on all people is the Biblical one. We have heard *ad nauseum* from these very same proponents that religious Jews and Christians have no right to impose their morality on society; in the view of the "politically correct" types, that right belongs only to themselves. The Bible at least claims God as its authority, but we are expected to accept politically correct morality based on nothing but the opinions of politically correct people.

The cause of "gay rights" is, of course, central to political

WINNING THROUGH INTIMIDATION

"Those who disagree with any objective of homosexual advocates -- or simply think it wrong to use other people's children to engage in social or political indoctrination -- are perilously close to losing the right to even voice their concerns on this issue. All opposition to homosexuality or homosexual political objectives is routinely viewed now as 'homophobia,' and many would designate all such speech 'hate crime.'"

M. Durham, Parents and Teachers for Responsible Schools, "First AIDS Education, Then 'Safe Schools,' Then Gay Advocacy," *NARTH Bulletin*, April 1998.

"At a later stage of the media campaign for gay rights -- long after other gay ads have become commonplace -- it will be time to get tough with remaining opponents. To be blunt, they must be vilified....Our goal here is twofold. First, we seek to replace the mainstream's self-righteous pride about its homophobia with shame and guilt. Second, we intend to make the anti-gays look so nasty that average Americans will want to dissociate themselves from such types."

Marshall Kirk and Erastus Pill, "The Overhauling of Straight America," *Guide Magazine*, November, 1987.

correctness. In communities where political correctness holds sway, all of its coercive power is brought to bear on dissenters who oppose the view that "gay" is good. However, despite efforts by the "gay" movement to criminalize anti-"gay" speech (so far limited to hate crimes statutes) the only power homosexualists currently have to enforce politically correct doctrines is intimidation. It follows that anyone who refuses to be intimidated is entirely free to oppose homosexuality in his own home and in society as a whole. It is up to you to prevent the "gay" movement from imposing its distorted version of morality on your child!

Take Inspiration From Traditional Morality

You don't have to be a Christian, a Jew or a Moslem (the three religions which are rooted in the Bible) to confidently use traditional moral guidelines about sexuality for your family. After thousands of years of successfully guiding civilization, these guidelines stand a much better chance of leading your child through a happy life than do the recently invented, self-serving theories of sexual freedom pushed by the "gay" movement and other libertine elements of society. Simply put, traditional sexual morality limits sex to monogamous, heterosexual, family-centered marriage. This standard is known as the Judeo-Christian sexual ethic.

You Don't Have to Be Morally "Spotless" to Promote Traditional Values to Your Child

One of the common misconceptions about traditional morality is that people who preach it must be perfectly morally pure: if they're not, then they are hypocrites. This notion constitutes an impossible standard — no one can measure up to such a level of perfection. (Consider that those who preach sexual freedom are beyond such criticism, since they have no standard at all.) The accusation of hypocrisy is frequently used to intimidate traditionalists and to discourage others from looking favorably at traditional morality.

TESTIMONIAL

"For many years I told people I was just born gay. It was the easy way to get people to accept us. If we were born gay that took away any personal responsibility for our behavior and made people feel sorry for us. All along though, we knew it was a convenient lie, but who could challenge it since it was our word against theirs. I love and respect myself today, but I hate the things that I used to do....Today I am living proof that homosexuals can and do change. I was as deep in the lifestyle as anyone. I spent nine years in one relationship and even thought about getting "married." I was 100% "gay," now I am 100% recovered...They call it Gay, but I can't think of a more miserable way of life.

Every time I hear someone talk approvingly of homosexuality, or see them go along with the idea of "gay rights" it breaks my heart, because I know it's like slamming the escape door on so many. It is especially painful to watch the radical gays manipulate their own parents and relatives into endorsing the gay political agenda. It's been several years since I left the gay lifestyle, but after watching the media constantly promote the lies and misinformation in favor of the homosexual way of life, I feel that I can't stay silent any more. It's time for someone who knows the real truth from the "inside" to step forward and tell it like it is. I am just one of many hundreds of ex-gays in Oregon. Perhaps if I set the example, they will also step forward and give people the truth.

Richard "Jonah" Weller, handbill, "The Voice They Want Silenced: *A former homosexual man speaks out about homosexuality and the politics of dishonesty,*" 1992.

Anyone who stops to think about it for a moment will recognize that an ideal is never diminished by a person's failure to live up to it. The ideal of monogamous, heterosexual, family-centered marriage is not made less valuable or desirable just because someone who promotes the ideal gets divorced, or cheats on his or her spouse, or carries on a sexual relationship before marriage. Certainly it hurts the credibility of the *person* promoting the ideal if it appears that he doesn't believe what he preaches, but his personal conduct has absolutely nothing to do with the worth or the validity of the ideal itself.

On the other hand, some of the best advice we can get about ideals is from people who have *not* lived up to them. Consider the value of the advice given by the still-addicted lifetime cigarette smoker with emphysema who preaches against the dangers of smoking, or of the prison inmates who try to get touring groups of troubled youths "scared straight" by showing the results of failure to live up to the ideal of good citizenship. The point here is that using your mistakes as an example, even sometimes when you are still living in the circumstances created by the mistake, can actually reinforce your credibility.

The Better Approach

Let us be very clear. In teaching healthy sexual morality to children there is no substitute for setting a good personal example. A parent's example may be the single most important factor in a child's decisions about his or her own conduct. However, it is likely that many people who read this book are parents whose sexual conduct sets a bad example, not a good one. If this is true of you, don't compound the problem by letting your personal failures (and the fear of being called a hypocrite) prevent you from teaching the ideal of traditional sexual morality to your child. If your example has been a poor one, you can at least let your child know that you want something better for him or her. Such a message in conjunction with an honest effort to set your own house in order could have a very powerful influence in your child's life. In any

NAME CALLING

"Homophobia....The very term 'phobia' ridicules our enemies (and intentionally so)."

"Gay" activists Marshall Kirk and Hunter Madsen, *After the Ball*, p. xxiv, 1990.

"Thoughtful people with a moderately healthy backbone are no longer intimidated by the charge of 'homophobia.' Along with the epithets of 'racism' and 'sexism,' the charge has lost its force by promiscuous overuse. Not everywhere, to be sure. In most colleges and universities thirty years ago, a faculty member who publicly announced that he thought homosexuality a good thing would have invited suspicion and censure. In the same schools today, he is likely in deep trouble if he offers less than unqualified approval of the homosexual movement. So there is no doubt that the insurgency has made advances. But we would be making a very big mistake if we measured cultural change by fashions in the academy."

Richard John Neuhaus, "Homosexuality and American Public Life," quoted in *NARTH Bulletin*, December 1997.

case, if you allow yourself to be intimidated into denying the ideal for fear of what other people think, the biggest loser will be your child.

Reject "Gay-Speak"

"Gay-speak" is the language of "gay" propaganda. As it relates to those who oppose homosexuality, "gay-speak" is a tool of intimidation and manipulation. Take, for example, the word "homophobia." Homophobia is a psychiatric term which means fear of the possibility that one might be homosexual oneself. In recent years the "gay" movement invented a new meaning for the word and began using it as a tool to silence its critics. The new meaning of homophobia is "an irrational fear and/or hatred of homosexuals." A "homophobe" is someone afflicted with homophobia. Through constant repetition in the popular culture by homosexualists, "homophobe" and "homophobia" have virtually become household words. Consider what the "gay" movement has gained by this tactic. For the first time, "gays" have a popularly accepted derogatory term for people who oppose homosexuality (at a time when it is absolutely socially forbidden to use any such term for homosexuals). Their new pejorative, at least subliminally, connects the person being described with homosexuality. (It is a favorite tactic of "gay" activists to imply that their opponents are themselves latent homosexuals.) More importantly, the accused "homophobe" must then rebut both the express accusation of being hateful toward homosexuals and the more subtly implied suggestion of mental illness (irrational fear). The "gay" movement has used this term to put opponents on the defensive, and even to suggest that there is no such thing as a reasonable opposition to homosexual behavior, only an irrational one.

Don't Let Yourself Be Put On The Defensive

If you take any public stand against homosexuality, no matter how pure your motive, be prepared for the accusation that you hate

"**Homophobia...is another form of gender bias adults teach young children ....educators have a serious responsibility to find ways to prevent and counter the damage before it becomes too deep.**"

Anti-Bias Curriculum, pp. 3-5.

June 29 - July 6, 1995   New England's Lar

Hate crimes bill passes Mass. House

Measure would make anti-gay bias crimes a felony

by Susan Ryan-Vollmar

"Portray gays as victims, not as aggressive challengers. In any campaign to win over the public, gays must be cast as victims in need of protection so that straights will be inclined by reflex to assume the role of protector. If gays are presented, instead, as a strong and prideful tribe promoting a rigidly nonconformist and deviant lifestyle, they are more likely to be seen as a public menace that justifies resistance and oppression. For that reason, we must forego the temptation to strut our 'gay pride' publicly when it conflicts with the Gay Victim image. And we must walk the fine line between impressing straights with our great numbers, on the one hand, and sparking their hostile paranoia -- 'They are all around us!' -- on the other."

Marshall Kirk & Erastes Pill, "The Overhauling of Straight America," *Guide Magazine*, November 1987.

homosexuals. In a one-on-one conversation or debate, the accusation usually takes the form of a direct question: "Why do you hate homosexuals?" Don't get tricked into answering that question or into believing that you must prove that you don't hate homosexuals. "Why do you hate homosexuals?" is not a genuine question, it is a rhetorical tactic designed to change the subject and put you on the defensive. Another familiar version of this tactic is the question, "Have you stopped beating your wife?" In the courtroom such a tactic is called "assuming facts not in evidence" and will always be thrown out by the judge upon a proper objection by the other side. There is almost no way to respond to such a question without hurting your credibility with anyone listening to the argument, because the question plants the suggestion in the listener's mind that a case against your character has already been proved. What is worse, if you fall into the trap, you will have allowed your opponent to change the subject — from a focus on the unacceptability of homosexuality to a focus on your character.

One effective response to "Why do you hate homosexuals?" is to turn the tables on your opponent and immediately say "Here's a better question. Why do you hate my child?" If simple moral opposition to homosexuality is presumed to be evidence of hatred, it is certainly no less reasonable to suggest that pushing the destructive "gay" lifestyle on children is even better evidence of hatred. Another way to respond is to unmask the tactic for what it is. You respond, "You're trying to change the subject and plant the suggestion that any opposition to homosexuality is hateful. Opposition to homosexuality is not hateful and I'm not going to let you change the subject. The subject is..."

You must recognize that no amount of evidence of how "nice" and how "goodhearted" you are will prevent you from being attacked as hateful for opposing homosexuality. The accusation has nothing to do with evidence. It is a tactic designed to cause you pain and embarrassment so that you will compromise your values or be silent. Incidentally, if confrontation on such a subject does cause you pain, it is a pain that we hope you will be willing to endure for the sake of your child.

THE APA'S SLIPPERY SLOPE:
HOMOSEXUALITY TO SADO-MASOCHISM TO PEDOPHILIA

"Dear Leather-S/M-Fetish Community Member,
    Some time ago The DSM Project was formed to organize efforts to modify the language of the Diagnostic and Statistical Manual of Mental Disorders (referred to as the DSM). This is the book which psychotherapeutic professionals usually refer to when seeking guidance in diagnosing mental illness. Until now, the DSM has considered sexual sadism, sexual masochism and fetishism to always be mental illnesses...The latest DSM (DSM-IV) has just been published and the new diagnostic criteria for sexual sadism, sexual masochism and fetishism no longer require mental health professionals to classify us as disturbed...Do not be fooled that attitudes about our style of sexuality will change overnight. Homosexuality was removed from the DSM as a mental illness more than two decades ago, but some psychotherapeutic professionals still persist with their biases against homosexuality....I would like to thank...Guy Baldwin, M.S., the individual who planted the seed for The DSM Project with his initial efforts of organizing kinky-friendly psychotheraputic professionals....Our community certainly has cause to celebrate."

Open letter to The International S/M Leather-Fetish Celebration, Race Bannon [a pseudonym taken from the children's cartoon Jonny Quest], *The DSM Project*, from an Oregon "gay" magazine (probably 1992).

"In the earlier DSM-III-R, pedophilia was diagnosed as a disorder if "[t]he person has acted out on these urges or is markedly distressed by them...but the new standard defines pedophilia as a disorder only if the fantasies, sexual urges, or behavior cause clinically significant distress or impairment in social, occupational, or other important areas of functioning."

Alan Medinger, *Regeneration News*, September, 1994.

Be Wary Of "Experts"

Homosexualists will typically rebut a parent's commonsense objections to homosexuality by invoking "experts" in the mental health field who assert that "gay" is normal. These people often point to the fact that homosexuality was removed from the American Psychiatric Association's (APA) official list of disorders in 1973. This victory for the "gay" movement, however, was not the result of any scientific breakthrough, but of intra-organizational politics. Homosexuality gained "normalcy" by a *vote* of APA members which was largely organized and controlled by "gay" activists. APA members who opposed the change were intimidated and harassed in a manner that is now recognized as a standard operating procedure for the "gay" movement. The APA vote did not make homosexuality any less of a disorder. It only changed the official policy of the association.

In casting their votes, the psychiatrists who voted to "normalize" homosexuality had to ignore most of the scientific evidence available at the time, including the results of the successful treatment of many homosexuals. To show how far the APA has drifted from reality under the continuing control of homosexualists, the organization has also voted to "normalize" sadomasochism and pedophilia. We bring this up not to make a case against the APA, but simply to forewarn you of a commonly used rhetorical tool of homosexualists: if there is no evidence to support the claim that homosexuality is normal, create your own evidence and then act as if it came from a reliable independent source. Throughout the writings of the homosexual advocacy movement you will find many references to such "end-justifies-the-means" tactics.

This book suggests that parents should avoid getting into a war of "experts," polls or statistics when dealing with homosexuals. It's not that opponents of homosexuality lack strong evidence and compelling documentation to back their position. On the contrary, the documentation provided throughout this book will prove valuable to anyone who decides to take on this issue as a community

THE GAY MIND

"I know that boy loving is a crime, but sodomy in Georgia is also a crime. So, should gay men stop having sex in Georgia because the government prohibits this?"

Editorial, *San Francisco Sentinel*, March 26, 1992.

"In homosexual philosophy, 'The self-evident truths' of the equality theory of civil rights have been replaced by the self-refuting claims of the diversity theory of civil rights....Its standard of relativism mandates logical nonsense. Everything is relative, except relativism. Everything must be tolerated except intolerance. To prevent the law from imposing morality, law must operate exclusively on the morality of cultural relativism and reject (other) claims to universal moral standards. The only absolute truth is that there is no absolute truth. It is evil to judge anyone's practices as evil."

Constitutional law scholar and civil rights attorney, David Llewellyn, "All Diversity Is Not Alike: Confronting Homosexuality In Law And Culture," p. 2, 1995.

39

activist. *As a parent, however, you do not need to prove anything to anybody to justify protecting your child from homosexuality.* Your authority resides in your role as a parent and in the self-evident truth that heterosexuality is the most fulfilling and natural sexual relationship for human beings. In other words, when it comes to your child, you are the only expert needed. If you find yourself battling over studies and statistics you will be fighting for ground you already hold. Some truths don't need special proof, a bare assertion is enough. Your inherent authority over your child, your role as the child's advocate and protector, is one such truth.

Don't Expect Logic and Facts to Persuade Homosexualists to Your View

Among the ancient Greek philosophers was a group called the Sophists, who were Western civilization's original moral relativists (i.e. they believed that all truth is relative and nothing is absolute). The Sophists were professional debaters whose goal was to persuade others to their point of view by any argument, truthful or not. To this day, sophism is defined as a false argument having the appearance of truth, and sophistry is defined as subtly false reasoning. "Gay" activists are modern America's leading sophists, dedicated to legitimizing their lifestyle at any cost, regardless of what may be best for our society and our children.

The "gay" movement's response to AIDS is a prime example. In the almost two decades in which the death rate of homosexual men from AIDS has soared, not a single "gay" leader has suggested publicly that young people should be discouraged from entering the "gay" lifestyle or from participating in anal sodomy, the principle means of AIDS transmission (and the reason why "gay" men have the highest and lesbians the lowest rates of infection). On the contrary, the "gay" movement has used the epidemic, as well as multiple millions of dollars in AIDS funding, as an opportunity to gain access to schoolchildren and to propagandize them. Many of our children then began receiving highly explicit and occasionally pornographic sex education instruction under the banner of "AIDS

THE VICTIM-PLUNDER STRATEGY

"Victim-plunder ideology is at the core of 'gay' political strategy. Homosexualists exploit the public [victim] status of homosexuals to impose their new definition of human sexuality upon society....Today's new victims see no reason to modify their own behavior....[They] have no true idea of how to act in the best interests of their country and fellow man. Their intention is to serve none but themselves."

[In victim-plunder ideology, victims of oppression or injustice are held to be entitled to retaliate against their oppressors; to be free to "plunder" society with impunity as a form of "reparations" for past injuries. Such an attitude explains why society is expected to tolerate disruptive civil disobedience by AIDS activists but is not expected to tolerate similar activity by anti-abortion demonstrators. (In "politically correct" circles, AIDS activists are considered to be victims, but anti-abortion activists are not).]

Kevin E. Abrams, from the Foreword to *The Pink Swastika: Homosexuality in the Nazi Party* by Scott Lively and Kevin E. Abrams, 1997.

"This essay is outre, madness, a tragic, cruel fantasy, an erruption of inner rage, on how the oppressed dream of becoming the oppressor ....We shall be victorious because we are filled with the ferocious bitterness of the oppressed..."

Michael Swift, "Gay Revolutionary," *Gay Community News*, February 15-21, 1987.

prevention." Unlimited student access to free condoms in some school districts is another by-product of the successful sale of AIDS propaganda to school administrators.

To "gay" activists, the end really does justify the means, and the truth is nothing but an obstacle to be overcome, if it conflicts with the "gay" political agenda. Not every homosexual puts his own interests ahead of the interests of children or society, but as a whole, the "gay" movement has repeatedly demonstrated by its actions that it is thoroughly Machiavellian.

Don't Tolerate Moral Outrage in Defense of Immorality

People who believe that homosexuality is normal may react with "moral outrage" to claims such as we have made in the preceding section. We have confidently claimed that the "gay" movement is guilty of cynically manipulating (or outright dispensing with) the truth in order to promote its agenda. This claim is logically consistent, in our view, because of the intrinsic "moral" position of American homosexuals relative to their own culture. In order to become openly and unapologetically homosexual, a person must forcefully reject one of the central tenets of Judeo-Christian morality, the sexual ethic. The sense of having stepped out of the boundaries of one's moral culture tends to translate into a general rejection of many of its other principles, including truthfulness. Thus, for many homosexual advocates, there is nothing wrong with deception in the service of their cause, since deception is only condemned by a morality they reject. However, the "gay" movement cannot have it both ways. It cannot reject traditional morality on the one hand, and then claim its protections on the other. In other words, homosexualists forfeit any right to evince "moral outrage" at being denied the presumption of truthfulness. By the same token they cannot evince "moral outrage" in defense of an immoral sexual lifestyle. Any claims to morality rest with the traditional moral culture and cannot logically be granted to those who reject that culture.

You as a parent, assuming you accept the traditional morality,

THE JUDEO-CHRISTIAN VIEW OF SEXUALITY

"Both Judaism and Christianity insist that there is a divinely ordained right order of things, and that our sexual drives find appropriate expression within that order in monogamous heterosexual unions. Only in the quite recent past has that millennia-old understanding come into question. It takes no extraordinary perception to see that God made men and women for each other; indeed it takes remarkable perversity of mind to get around that obvious intent. Homosexuals have the right to expect of the rest of us decent and respectful treatment as human beings and citizens; they have no right to insist that we surrender our fundamental moral and religious beliefs in order that they might feel comfortable with their sexual behavior."

First Things, November 1990.

Select Biblical Passages On
Sexuality and Homosexuality

Sex is good: Proverbs 5:18, Song of Solomon 4:5, 7:1, 6-9.

Intended only for marriage: Genesis 2:24, Proverbs 5:15-17.

All created heterosexual: Genesis 5:2, Hebrews 13:4.

Other sex acts banned: Leviticus 18:6-30, I Thessalonians 4:3.

Condemnation of homosexuality: Genesis 19:4-13, Leviticus 18:22, Judges 19:22-30, I Kings 15:9-12, Romans 1:18-32, I Corinthians 6:9, I Timothy 1:10, Jude 1:4-7.

do have the right to moral outrage in defense of your child. Don't be cowed by those who claim moral authority with nothing to back it up but their own opinions. Indeed, it is within your moral authority to condemn such a tactic.

You Don't Have to Be Religious, Just Righteous

There is no requirement that you be "religious" in order to take an active role in shielding your children from "gay" recruitment. You can, however, be *righteous* in your attitude and your arguments, whether you are religious or not. Righteousness is simply doing what is right, acting with the courage of your convictions. Righteousness is an important quality of leadership; it inspires our children when they see it in others and it will inspire them when they see it in us. If you are not a religious person, you don't have to become one to be righteous in defense of your child, but it would be very useful if you became familiar with some of the Biblical teachings about sexuality. Our recommended passages are listed on the opposite page.

Take Authority *Today* to Protect Your Child

Thus far we have introduced the most important issues related to taking authority on behalf of your child. It is up to you to follow up these suggestions and admonitions with further research and study. We have provided a list of resources that will help you become better informed on these and other issues which have to do with homosexuality. We hope you will investigate some of these. We also encourage you to adopt a deeply questioning attitude towards the messages on homosexuality that pour out of the entertainment and news media, the NEA-approved sex-education curricula, and the liberal political establishment. Where do these messages originate? On what authority do their claims rest? Do such claims stand up to the test of your experience and common sense? Remember that we are living in an era of propaganda, in which "spin" and intimidating attitudes are often used to push ideas

AN OUNCE OF PREVENTION...

"There is no such penalty for error and folly than to see one's children suffer for it."

W. G. Sumner

"During a certain period (usually shortly before adolescence and in early adolescence) children prefer members of their own sex. Boys look down on girls, have male heroes, and enjoy being together, while girls 'detest' boys, have crushes on girls, and love some 'best friend' intensely. With the coming of sexual maturity, their sexual drives are, not always without conflict, directed toward members of the opposite sex. During this difficult period, unfortunate experiences may have a devastating effect on certain young people, namely those who have emotional problems. These experiences, whether subtle or obvious, form a barrier on the road of normal sexual development. Homosexuality is a detour on that highway, and some people never find their way back to the main road, especially if their homosexuality has brought additional problems of guilt and fear to confuse them."

Benjamin F. Miller, M.D., *The Complete Medical Guide* (revised) p. 187.

which are contrary to the values and good sense of the audience. It is very difficult to stand alone against the tactics of political correctness, but the odds change when you have even one other parent who shares your concerns and is willing to stand with you in your efforts. And remember that the promoters of politically correct opinions about homosexuality do not have the best interests of *your own child* at heart. You do. Do whatever it takes to protect that child.

Photo courtesy of Traditional Values Coalition

"The idea that people are born into one type of sexual behavior is entirely foolish, says Dr. John DeCecco, Psychology Professor at San Francisco State University and editor of the Journal of Homosexuality. Homosexuality, he says, is a behavior, not a condition, and something that some people can and do change, just like they sometimes change their other tastes and personality traits."

USA Today, January 1, 1990.

Step Three

Inform Yourself

PART ONE: THE "GAY" IDENTITY

"Gay" Is How You Act, Not Who You Are

In the behavior-based view of homosexuality which was dominant before the "gay" movement invented the sexual orientation theory, categories of sexual types made sense. If a man engaged in homosexuality, he was called a homosexual. If he molested boys he was called a pederast (pederasty is a form of pedophilia which involves sex between adult men and boys or adolescents). If he participated in what is called "rough trade" he was called a sadomasochist (one who derives sexual pleasure from inflicting and receiving pain). If he engaged in all three he was at once a homosexual, a pederast *and* a sadomasochist in the same way that one can at once be a carpenter, a plumber and an electrician — in other words, he was defined by his behavior. *All* people were assumed to be heterosexuals, each with the capacity to choose to participate in any possible form of sexual deviance. The sexual behavior model was a completely logical, consistent, and objective standard which any person with actual knowledge of the facts could apply.

ORIENTATION TOWARDS YOUTH

"In another article, 'The Main Thing is Being Wanted: Some Case Studies on Adult Sexual Experiences with Children,' the author says that one-third of the pedophiles he has studied claimed that 'their sexual desire for children is a natural part of their constitution. This desire is variously described as 'inbred,' 'innate,' 'a fact of nature,' 'inherent in them,' etc. the *leitmotif* of their accounts is 'this is me' or 'just the way I am.'

The author concludes that the feeling of being 'born a pedophile' makes them feel they cannot change, and therefore they are convinced they have the same right as other people to pursue the 'natural' expression of their sexuality. The same author quotes a respondent's belief that "if adult-child sex was commonplace, the majority of it would surely be good for both participants."

Journal of Homosexuality (vol. 20, nos. 1/2, 1990), quoted In *NARTH Bulletin*, December 1997.

"The love between men and boys is at the foundation of homosexuality. For the gay community to imply that boy-love is not homosexual love is ridiculous. We in the gay community...need to support the men and boys in those relationships."

Editorial, *San Francisco Sentinel*, March 26, 1992.

Under sexual orientation theory, however, people are categorized based on the focus of their sexual desire. If the focus of their desire is always someone of the same gender they are called homosexual. If the focus of their desire is sometimes a man and sometimes a woman, they are called bisexual. If the focus of their desire is always someone of the opposite sex they are called heterosexual. So far the theory seems somewhat reasonable, but beyond this point it becomes absurdly unreasonable. There is very little logic, for example, to the way in which sexual orientations are categorized. A man's sexual desire to dress in women's clothing is called a sexual orientation (such a person is designated "transgendered"), but an adult's desire to engage in sex with children, or in sadomasochism, or in bestiality (sex with animals) or in various other well-known sexual behaviors is not. The only basis for this distinction seems to be political. Sexual orientation categories appear to be determined by whether their members belong to one of the "gay," "lesbian," "bisexual" or "transgendered" subgroups of the "gay" political movement.

The "Sexual Orientation" Shell Game

One sometimes hears the argument that pedophilia and bestiality are not sexual orientations because they are against the law. This makes no sense at all. Would they suddenly become sexual orientations if they were legalized? Is homosexuality *not* an orientation in places where it is illegal? Scientific truth, which sexual orientation theory claims to be, does not depend on legal status. Furthermore, if sexual orientation is not based on behavior, but only on sexual desire, what difference does it make whether the behavior is legal or not? A private desire to have sex with children or animals (if it is never expressed or acted upon in any way) has exactly the same impact on society as the private unexpressed desire for homosexuality or normal heterosexual intercourse — none!

On the other hand, sadomasochism is not illegal. Why isn't the "gay" movement willing to classify sadomasochism as an "orientation" based on the criterion of sexual desires? The answer is

THE UPSIDE-DOWN MORAL UNIVERSE

"The time has come for someone to call this sexual re-formation into question, and try to de-code the clever rationalizations worked out by gay and lesbian politicians to lessen their own psychic pain. If there's one thing I know as a psychoanalyst, I know this: people don't get to the bottom of their pain by lying about it, to themselves or to the world -- much less by creating what a critic of the movement calls 'an upside down moral universe,' which is just another way of saying a general, community-wide dementia."

Charles W. Socarides, M.D. Homosexuality- A Freedom Too Far. p. 13. 1995.

"[We at Regeneration] believe that homosexuality is a developmental condition....We do not deny, however, that some children, by personality type or other inborn characteristics, may be more vulnerable to homosexuality than others. Neither do we deny that there is an element of free will in the development of homosexuality; not that a child chooses to be homosexual, but that the child chooses to respond to his or her less than perfect environment in ways that can lead to homosexuality."

Alan Medinger, "How to Raise a Heterosexual Child," *Regeneration News*, November, 1992.

that sadomasochism (like pedophilia and bestiality) is a behavior so unacceptable to most people that they would not go along with legitimizing it just because the people who do it might have been "born that way" or might have been influenced by biological factors. If the public were to decide in one case that the existence of an orientation should not automatically mean social acceptance for the behavior connected with it, they might apply the very same logic to the homosexual orientation. The "gay" movement cannot afford this kind of association. Society might decide that homosexual *orientation* is acceptable, but at the same time decide that homosexual *behavior* should be discouraged. Homosexualists would rather be illogical and count on the power of political correctness to discourage people from unmasking their deception.

Homosexuals Are *Not* a "Third Sex"

It is apparent that sexual orientation theory is nothing but a political doctrine masquerading as scientific truth. Its goal is to foster the belief that homosexuality is a normal form of sexuality that occurs naturally in human beings. Homosexualists cleverly deceive many people by crafting their rhetoric so that this conclusion is assumed as a fact. For example, when one talks about various forms of bizarre sexual behavior which are common in the "gay" lifestyle, the response is, "Heterosexuals do that, too." This innocent-seeming retort hides a very subtle deception. It assumes as a fact the premise that homosexuality is a natural state of being, equal to and exclusive of heterosexuality, and that homosexuality is not itself deviance from a heterosexual norm. The statement implies that both homosexuals and heterosexuals enjoy a comparable status not defined by behavior, but that both groups indulge equally in various fetishes. *In reality, homosexuality is just another form of sexual deviance practiced by heterosexuals, it is not the natural sexual expression of a "third sex" of human beings called homosexuals.* In other words, *all* people are naturally heterosexual in design, but some engage (occasionally or all the time) in one or more types of sexual deviance: homosexuality, pedophilia,

DEVIATING FROM THE NORM

"I believe that we are all heterosexual, but that some people have a homosexual problem."

Dr. Joseph Nicolosi, *NARTH Bulletin*, August, 1997.

"Homosexual behavior is unnatural. It is a perversion of the obvious intended use of the sexual and excretory organs. Homosexual couples are not the moral or sociological equivalent of natural families. They rarely practice sexual fidelity. They rarely remain together for a lifetime, as well over 50% of heterosexual married couples do. They rarely produce children, for whose protection society has adopted extensive family laws. Their conduct, unlike marriage and sex within marriage, performs no beneficial social function which would entitle them to legal protections; on the contrary, homosexual practices impose detrimental financial and administrative costs on employers, insurers, taxpayers and medical providers....Practices so obviously tied to personal and public health problems such as AIDS and numerous other sexually transmitted diseases should reasonably be regulated, restricted, or prohibited altogether, not considered for special civil rights protections."

David Llewellyn, "Logical Opposition To Homosexual Rights, *Life & Liberty*, 1994.

sadomasochism and so on. To accept without challenge the assertion that "heterosexuals do that, too" is to grant undeserved legitimacy to sexual orientation theory.

Don't Be Intimidated by the Word "Deviant"

Deviance is a condition or a status that exists only in reference to a standard or norm. Homosexuality has always been called deviant because it *deviates* from the heterosexual norm. There is absolutely nothing wrong with labeling homosexuality deviant if you recognize that heterosexuality is *the* norm for human beings. Indeed, it is important for parents to use the term when they speak about homosexuality for the very reason that homosexualists *don't* want it to be used: it reminds us all that a standard exists by which to measure sexual behavior. The fact that the word has pejorative connotations shows that its meaning is rooted in the history of a society deeply committed to preserving the family and its corollary, heterosexual normalcy, and to discouraging behaviors which threaten it.

Homosexuality Cannot Be "Normal"

One of the most baffling questions about the homosexual issue is how so many people can blindly accept the notion that homosexuality is a normal variant of human sexuality. This is especially puzzling considering that each one of us is either male or female, and that all of our sexual drives are tied in some way to our heterosexual reproductive functions. We talk about "raging hormones," "chemistry" and various biological "cycles" playing their roles in people's sex lives. Isn't it obvious that every one of these biological influences is linked to reproduction? Do people think it is merely a coincidence that a woman's sexual drive is linked to her menstrual cycle or that male orgasm occurs at the point of ejaculation of sperm? The links between drives, pleasure and reproduction helps to ensure the very survival of the human race. Certainly there is an overtly recreational aspect to our sexuality, but

Background: "Scientist" Dean Hamer exposed in *London Daily Mail*.
Foreground: "Objective" brain researcher, Simon LeVay, and young friend launch a "gay and lesbian" study center in West Hollywood, CA.

the self-evident purpose of sexual impulse and sexual pleasure, even in non-human species, lies in the biological mandate to perpetuate the race. For homosexuality to be normal, in the sense that heterosexuality is normal, it would have to serve some function in human procreation. Obviously it does not.

It has been suggested that homosexuality serves a reproduction-related function, as a built-in protection from overpopulation. However, as we are so often reminded by the "gay" movement, homosexuals have been with us since the beginning of civilization — through hundreds of centuries when *under*population, not overpopulation, was the constant threat to human survival.

Are Homosexuals "Born That Way?": Science vs. Propaganda.

Despite much media hype about "gay" genes, no one has ever proved a biological cause for homosexuality. In every case, those who have claimed to have discovered proof have been discredited when their research has come under the scrutiny of non-"gay" scientists. Although the news media gives wide exposure to the initial claims of these researchers, reporters are less zealous about informing the general public that the original claims they heard of "gay" brain structures, "gay" genes and so on were later debunked. In nearly every case, the authors of these discredited studies have been unmasked as "gay" political activists. For example, after publishing his now thoroughly repudiated study on "gay" brains, researcher Simon Levay went on to open a school for "gay" studies. Dean Hamer, author of a widely heralded "gay" gene study, later became the object of an investigation of scientific fraud. Because of these incidents, many people have come to believe that the purpose of "gay" science is to produce propaganda rather than to further our knowledge about what causes homosexuality.

THE IMPOSSIBLE "GAY" GENE

"Those who contend that homosexuality is genetic have a series of hurdles to leap to prove their point scientifically....evolutionary mechanisms maintain and expand favorable genetic mutations because they convey some sort of net advantage. . . .[but] what is the net advantage of being a homosexual or engaging in homosexuality?....Try as we might, documenting even *one* evolutionary advantage to the homosexual lifestyle seems impossible, and calculating a net advantage from homosexuality is daunting indeed....[Additionally] *very* few homosexuals have children....So even if homosexuals have some advantage to pass on to their children, not very many homosexuals can do any passing, because they don't have kids....Not only do fewer homosexuals have children, but when they do reproduce, homosexuals also tend to have fewer children....[And what of the incidence of homosexuality among these children?] various gay researchers claims to have proven that the natural children of homosexuals are no more apt to become homosexual than children raised by heterosexuals....With this bit of information, the genetic theory of homosexuality disintegrates....taken at their word, unlike all other kinds of parents, homosexuals are monumentally unsuccessful in passing on their unique characteristic to their few children."

Dr. Paul Cameron, "Homosexuality Can't Be Genetic," *Family Research Report*, November-December 1993.

Defect or Design? Creation and Evolution Agree.

As demonstrated above, homosexuality is not "normal" in the sense that heterosexuality is normal, but that doesn't mean it has no biological cause. Further, proof of a biological cause would not necessarily imply that homosexuality occurs naturally in healthy humans. Physical deformities and congenital diseases are recognized as biologically caused *defects* in human beings. In the light of the fact that the human reproductive mandate is at the root of all human sexuality, any biological condition which could be demonstrated to promote homosexuality would have to be considered a defect at variance with the design of human beings. The facts lead to this conclusion whether one believes that humans are the creation of God or the product of evolution.

The theory of special creation, based on the Bible, states that men and women were created as heterosexual beings designed to live together in a covenant of marriage. They were commanded by God to shun all other sexual relationships under pain of His divine judgment. God would not have created a genetic condition which sabotaged His own design, nor would He have created an entire class of people with no choice but to engage in a behavior which He had condemned. On the contrary, the Bible specifically states that God gives each person free will and holds him accountable for his choices, even when temptation to do wrong may be heightened by biological factors which are beyond the person's control.

If the theory of evolution is true, any gene associated with homosexuality would tend to disappear from the gene pool in a relatively few generations, let alone the hundreds of thousands of generations which evolutionary theory requires for its time frame. Natural selection, which is the mechanism which makes evolution happen, favors only those factors which contribute to greater reproductive capacity (more offspring). Factors such as homosexuality, which make any given person less likely to reproduce, would logically be found in the gene pool with decreasing frequency. A person disinclined to have sexual relations with a member of the opposite sex would, over a lifespan, tend to

RECRUIT, RECRUIT, RECRUIT

"Editorializing the 1992 *Advocate*, Donna Minkowitz... proclaims herself 'increasingly impatient with the old chestnut that our movement for public acceptance has not increased and will not increase the number of gay men and lesbians in existence. There are more of us than there used to be...We have been on the defensive far too long....'phobes like Pat Robertson are right when they say that we threaten the family, male domination, and the Calvinist ethic of work and grimness that has paralyzed most Americans' search for pleasure.

Indeed, instead of proclaiming our innocuousness, we ought to advertise our potential to change straight society in radical, beneficial ways. Hets [sic] have much to learn from us: first and foremost, the fact that pleasure is possible (and desirable) beyond the sanctions of the state. Another fact gleaned from gay experience - that gender is for all intents and purposes a fiction - also has the potential to revolutionize straight lives....

Let's take the offensive for a change, whether the issue is promiscuity or recruiting the previously straight. Remember that most of the line about homosex [sic] being one's nature, not a choice, was articulated as a response to brutal repression....it's time for us to abandon this defensive posture and walk upright on the earth. Maybe you didn't choose to be gay - that's fine. But I did." The ultimate answer? "Recruit, recruit, recruit!"

Donna Minkowitz, quoted in Cameron, "Seduction as a cause," *Family Research Report*, November-December 1993.

produce fewer offspring than a person with heterosexual inclinations. If the "homosexual gene" *were* present, it would be passed to some of the offspring produced, and they in turn would produce fewer offspring than their heterosexual peers, and so on, tending ultimately to the extinction of the gene. In addition, we know that the lifespan of homosexuals (especially male homosexuals) is substantially shorter than that of their heterosexual counterparts due to the high rate of disease associated with homosexual practices. This would make a homosexual less able to contribute his genes to the next generation than someone who lived a long and reproductively active life. In short, if there ever were a genuine "homosexual gene" it would have become extinct long ago.

Recruitment Is a More Logical Explanation

The continuing presence of homosexuals in society over the centuries may be better explained as the result of recruiting. Such a phenomenon is familiar to us as the way that religions and even fraternal organizations perpetuate themselves. None of the members of these social institutions are "born that way," although their sense of identity may be very closely tied to membership in their group. Like homosexuals in the "gay" community, the members of these institutions are unified by common beliefs, interests, pursuits, goals and a sense of belonging to something larger than themselves. Some organizations, such as religious cults, may be even more closely analogous to the "gay" community in that the members may share a very close bond fostered by an "us versus them" mentality. People who share an identity as "outcasts" because of their actions or beliefs are especially susceptible to such feelings.

The membership of religious and fraternal organizations waxes and wanes over time based on how effectively they attract and keep (recruit) new members. Likewise, the size of the "gay" community has apparently also fluctuated in history. The "gay" population was very large in sexually decadent Greece, Rome and pre-Nazi Germany prior to the collapse of each, but was relatively low in

NATURE OR NURTURE?

"Those societies that discriminate against homosexuality have few or no homosexuals. Those that accept or ignore homosexuality have much more of it."

Dr. Paul Cameron, summarizing Christopher Hewitt's analysis of attitudes toward homosexuality and the frequency of homosexuality in various societies, *Family Research Report*, November/December 1993.

"We're born man, woman and sexual beings. We learn our sexual preferences and orientations."

Masters & Johnson, UPI, 4/23/79.

"Increasingly today, we are abandoning support of our boys' formation of masculine identity; particularly the support needed from the parents. For the boy, the father is most significant in the identification process. If he is warm and receptive and inviting, the boy will disidentify with mother and bond with father to fulfill his natural masculine strings. If the father is cold, detached, harsh, or even simply disinterested, the boy may reach out, but eventually will feel hurt and discouraged and surrender his natural masculine strivings, returning to his mother."

Dr. Joseph Nicolosi, "Gay as Self-Reinvention," *Narth Bulletin*, December 1997.

America prior to the 1960s. It is possible, but not likely, that the percentage of homosexuals in society has remained relatively constant and that homosexuals were simply reluctant to identify themselves in societies in which their behavior was frowned upon. However, many of these societies — including our own — actively prosecuted homosexuals criminally and thus record-keeping in the courts provides a rough indicator of the total number of homosexuals in the culture. Such records support the notion that the percentage of homosexuals in society remains quite small when the society does not condone homosexual behavior, thus limiting homosexuals' freedom to openly recruit new members. If homosexuality is not genetically transmitted, then a combination of environmental factors and homosexual recruitment is the most reasonable explanation for the persistent presence of homosexuals in human history, and for their greater or smaller numbers in different societies.

Environmental Influences in Childhood May Contribute to Homosexuality in Some People

Leading psychologists who treat homosexuality theorize that homosexual tendencies often result from environmental influences in early childhood. These therapists characterize homosexuality as a "gender identity dysfunction" produced by a child's failure to "bond" with his same-sex parent or parental surrogate during a critical phase of early childhood when gender, identity is formed. They believe that certain factors (such as a rejecting or emotionally or physically absent parent) can cause a child to reject his own gender and to subconsciously identify himself as a member of the opposite gender; that of the more emotionally trustworthy opposite-sex parent. According to the theory, a person's false gender identification affects every aspect of his emotional life, including his sexuality. A person with a gender identity disorder knows he is male or female but subconsciously perceives himself to be a member of the opposite sex and thus subconsciously perceives members of the same sex as the appropriate objects of his sexual

A DISABILITY BY ANY OTHER NAME

"Perhaps you saw it too, the story about this new organization of physically disabled people who criticize the movie actor Christopher Reeves because he wants to be cured. The group wants to promote what it calls disability pride. 'I can't walk and I'm glad I can't walk,' declared one young woman. 'I don't want to walk. Disability is good!' We must hope that she does not really believe that. While being sensitive to the poignancy of her defiance, we must refuse her demand that we believe that. Her disability is not good, it is very sad; but she is more than her disability. We support her in her struggle, and help her not at all by pretending that it is not a struggle.

Of that truth we must also persuade our homosexual brothers and sisters. We must do so in a way that carefully distinguishes between affirmation of the homosexual person and opposition to the homosexual movement. We must do so humbly, in painful awareness of our different, but often more severe disabilities. But we must also do so firmly, knowing that homosexuals are not helped and many lives are ruined by their effort to impose upon others their defiant denial of the troubling truth."

Richard John Neuhaus, "Homosexuality and American Public Life," quoted in *Narth Bulletin*, December 1997.

interest.

Many homosexual men, especially those with pronounced effeminate traits and mannerisms, have been successfully treated by therapists who subscribe to the theory of gender identity dysfunction. One treatment approach is called "reparative therapy." The theory of gender identity dysfunction can't explain all incidents of homosexuality, but it does explain why *some* homosexuals would sense that they were "born that way;" the development of their gender disorder (probably sometime before the age of three) would predate their earliest memories. We must distinguish here between the honest belief by some homosexuals that they were "born that way," and the "gay" movement's claim that *all* homosexuals are born "gay." The former, if the theory of gender identity disorder is true, is an honest but mistaken belief held by some but not all members of the "gay" community, the latter is a deliberate lie which is intended to mislead the general public and advance a political agenda.

If Homosexuals *Were* "Born That Way," Would It Really Matter?

An often unchallenged assumption of sexual orientation theory is that the fact of having been born "gay" justifies someone's homosexual behavior and limits society's right to regulate it. However, even if homosexuality *were* biologically based, society would still have both the right and the responsibility to regulate it. Society has an interest in regulating *any* behavior which affects the health, safety, welfare or morals of the community. Not even religious behavior, which enjoys the highest level of Constitutional protection in the United States under the First Amendment, is beyond state control when it conflicts with the basic needs of society. (The early Mormon religious practice of polygamy, for example, was held to be illegal in every State.)

We can understand why some people would accept the argument that a biological cause for homosexuality legitimizes homosexual behavior. Historically, it was commonly believed that

THE ALCOHOLISM GENE

"Initial findings by homosexual researchers [purporting to have found a 'gay' gene] with a clearly stated agenda were fed to a sympathetic press, which generously splashed these findings (and the alleged implications) across America's front pages....a comparison to the news media's handling of a similar genetic study will show how disproportionate the current hoopla really is. In the fall of 1991 (around the same time as LeVay's results were published), researchers at the City of Hope Medical Center found a certain gene to be present in 77 percent of alcoholics who were studied, yet absent in 72 percent of the nonalcoholics also studied. This presented significant evidence for a genetic predisposition toward alcoholism, which has long been a subject of interest and concern to Americans. Yet no major magazine featured these studies on their covers, and they received only passing mention in the press."

Former homosexual, Joe Dallas, "BORN GAY? How politics have skewed the debate over the biological causes of homosexuality." *Christianity Today*, June 22, 1992.

"Turning sensitive, impressionable teens and preteens over to practicing gay and lesbian counsellors...is like inviting drunken, unrecovered alcoholics to take teens to bars and teach them how to drink liquor."

Lou Sheldon, in New Dimentions, January 1990.

homosexuality was nothing more than a choice arising from moral weakness, like the choice to steal someone else's property. Public policy against homosexuality was defended in part on the grounds that homosexuals could easily choose not to engage in homosexual behavior. After homosexualists successfully sold the idea that homosexuals are "born that way" and are responding to an instinctual homosexual drive, there were people who concluded that social condemnation of homosexual behavior was no longer justified.

We find two major problems with this conclusion. First, public attitudes and policies against homosexuality are not based on the reasons for being homosexual, but on the destructive effects of the "gay" lifestyle on society and on homosexuals themselves. Such harmful effects as the spread of disease; the weakening of the concept of the nurturing, procreative family; the proliferation of the notion of sex without commitment or social responsibility; and the relentless efforts to proselytize the young on the merits of this personally devastating lifestyle; all these justify social attitudes and policies which discourage or limit the spread of homosexuality.

Second, a behavior is not legitimized by the mere discovery that it has a biological cause. Remember that homosexuality is *behavior*-based; it is not like skin color. Even if the causes of homosexuality come from the realm of biology, its effects are felt in the realm of social life. There are other examples of behavioral phenomena that are thought to have biological origins, and we will look at how society deals with one of them.

The Analogy of Homosexuality with Alcoholism

The phenomenon of alcoholism provides a helpful analogy in understanding why a biological cause does not legitimize homosexual behavior. There are many strong similarities between these two behavior-based lifestyles. Both homosexuality and alcoholism are conditions which affect large numbers of people from all walks of life, conditions which have traditionally been condemned by Western society. Up until this century, both have

CHOOSING TO BE "GAY"

"For starters, I personally don't think I was 'born this way.' (In fact, when I'm feeling hostile, I've been known to tell right-wingers that I'm a successfully "cured" hetero.) Until I was in my early thirties, I fell in love with men, took pleasure in sleeping with them, and even married one. But like most women, I experienced most of my closest emotional relationships with female friends. The only thing that made me different was that at some point I got curious about lesbian feminist claims that it was possible to combine that intense female intimacy with good sex. The good sex part turned out to be vastly easier than I anticipated. Even so, there was no immediate *biological* reason to stop having sex with men or to start living as a lesbian. Coming out was, for me, a conscious decision -- every step of the way.

...If there's anything we as feminists ought to be supporting, it's a frank, unapologetic celebration of sexual *choice*. I'm personally for the right of happy heterosexuals to 'experiment' with same-sex love and perhaps find that they like it. I'm for the right of bisexuals to opt for gay relationships, even though they don't have the excuse that they have no other choice. And I'm for the right of gay people to *choose* to act on their sexuality, whether society approves of it or not."

Lindsy Van Gelder, contributing editor to *Ms.* Magazine, "The 'Born That Way' Trap, *Ms.*, May/June 1991.

been perceived as choices born of moral weakness; now genetic factors are being claimed as possible causes of each. Both involve powerful compulsive drives and strongly addictive behavior. Both pose grave health risks which dramatically reduce the life expectancy of members of the group. Both conditions are characterized by the active practice of specific behaviors, but individual members may continue to identify themselves as homosexuals or alcoholics even during periods of abstinence. Finally, there are many former practitioners of each lifestyle whose new purpose in life is to help others to escape that lifestyle and find freedom from its compulsive behavior.

When we compare homosexuality to alcoholism, we can conclude that society has as much right to discourage "gay" behavior as it has to discourage alcohol addiction, even if both are genetically based. No one suggests that alcoholism should be legitimized because it may have roots in a person's biological make-up. No one suggests that society, or family members, would suffer less from the consequences of alcoholic behavior if alcoholism were found to be genetic.

The Homosexual's Choice

Debate over homosexuality usually centers on the question of whether or not it is a choice. To clear away the confusion on this issue, we must look closely at what it is that is being chosen. Homosexual activists often assert that they did not choose to be "gay," meaning that they did not choose to have homosexual desires, but only discovered such desires within themselves. Society's concern in the matter, however, is not whether one has homosexual desires, but whether one *acts* on those desires by engaging in homosexual behavior. Any consensual homosexual behavior, like all sexual behavior, clearly *is* a choice. In this sense, a homosexual's pursuit of the "gay" lifestyle is also a choice; it is a series of voluntary sexual encounters. As with any compulsive behavior, the overwhelming urge for gratification may make a homosexual *feel* that he has no choice, but he does. Here again we

68

"Our friends advised us that M. has been selected for the National Girls Initiative, where *young lesbians between the ages of nine and fifteen* will be photographed."

Patlar Magazine whose motto is Voice of Lesbian/Gay America, p. 32, October 1991. (Emphasis ours).

find the situation of the homosexual analogous to that of the alcoholic.

In the sense that a person trapped in homosexual behavior may protest that he did not choose to be "gay," the typical alcoholic did not choose to be a drunk. Yet, somewhere along the way, he wakes to the reality that he has become one. Each successive drinking binge involved a conscious choice to indulge himself. He didn't choose to *be* an alcoholic, he only chose to give in to his desires, one episode at a time. Later, when he began to want to escape from the alcoholic lifestyle he found it just wasn't that easy. The addiction to alcohol was overpowering. He certainly did not choose to become its slave. It always remained his choice, however, to stay trapped in his addiction or to fight his way back to health and wholeness.

It is important to reiterate that as far as society's interest goes, choice is relevant only in regards to the behavior that is chosen. As powerful as his addiction may be, an alcoholic cannot claim he has no choice. Neither can a homosexual, as thousands of ex-"gays" can attest.

PART TWO: THE "GAY" LIFESTYLE

Of all the special interest groups in this nation, only one defines itself by sexual preference: the "gay" community. The sole unifying characteristic of its members is the practice of homosexual sexual acts. What animates the "gay" community as a whole, if not every individual member, is an obsessive preoccupation with sexuality and eroticism (this is true of both male and female homosexuals but applies to males to a far greater degree). Such an assessment might seem overstated to those whose only knowledge of the "gay" movement comes from the mainstream media or casual familiarity with openly "gay" acquaintances. The public face of the "gay" community, however, is false; it is the product of public relations strategies and the careful suppression of unpleasant facts about life in the "gay" subculture. The face of "gay" life which reveals its behavioral component is far less benign.

One can get a glimpse behind the "gay" community's public

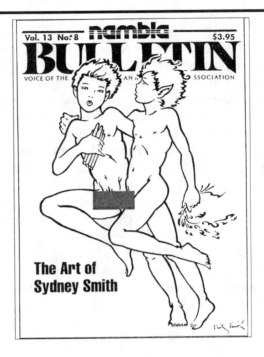

Vol. 13 No. 8 **nambla** $3.95
BULLETIN
VOICE OF THE ~~AN~~ ~~SSOCIATION~~

**The Art of
Sydney Smith**

"Childhood sexual seductions are an obvious cause of homosexuality. When these seductions give pleasure and comfort, the same-sex sex can become addictive, especially when it overtakes someone caught up in a traumatic family situation. The sex — so quick and easy — can help relieve a person's anxiety. Thus it becomes a kind of habit. Like any habit, smoking for instance, it is acquired by repeated acts. And, like smoking, it is a habit that can be hard to kick. That's the way it is with addictions that give great pleasure."

Charles Socarides M.D., *Homosexuality, A Freedom Too Far*, p. 19, 1995.

mask by skimming through any of the hundreds of "gay" newspapers and other publications which are readily found in big-city public libraries and community centers across the nation. The typical "gay" publication has the outward appearance of most such free periodicals. Look inside, however, and you will find that most articles relate in some way to sexual activity or "gay" politics (that is, organized efforts to legitimize homosexual activity). Many articles discuss with an air of comfortable familiarity sexual behaviors which most people would find deviant and disturbing in the extreme. Frankly pornographic images are scattered throughout the typical publication; these sometimes include explicit depictions of sodomy, sadomasochism, and group sex. Many publications contain page after page of graphic advertisements for phone sex and escort services; some of these, expressly or by implication, offer teenagers for sex. Some publications contain ads for America's largest openly pederastic organization, NAMBLA (the North American Man/Boy Love Association).

Homosexual publications give us a glimpse of the "gay" lifestyle and its obsessive sexual focus, but they do not tell the whole story. "Gay" editors know that their newspapers and magazines circulate, to a small extent, in the local community. Like the prison inmate who knows his phone calls are being monitored, "gay" editors reveal only what they believe cannot damage their political and social goals. Testimonies of those who have come out of the "gay" lifestyle (and some who remain trapped there) give us a better picture of the forces which drive and dominate homosexual practice.

Homosexuality and Sexual Addiction

The concept of sexual addiction helps to explain many aspects of the homosexual lifestyle. It is widely acknowledged today that sexual behavior is one of the areas of human behavior most susceptible to addiction (many of us know someone who is a heterosexual addict of pornography or extramarital sex). Central to the pattern of sexual addiction is the idea of sexual adventure, the

ONCE UNMENTIONABLE FOR ADULTS, NOW INSTRUCTIONAL FOR KIDS

"In New York City, the Gay Men's Health Crisis was able to invite school students to a workshop in February 1994, which they conducted. The GMHC used the school district's office space, faxes, people and mail network to promote the conference. They also used the name of the Board of Education, as if their conference were a school event. Parents were *excluded* from the conference. And for obvious reasons. Matters such as lesbian 'fisting,' 'golden showers' (sexual activity with urine), 'enemas,' 'welts' and 'blisters,' sexual use of 'crops,' 'whips,' and 'canes,' and 'anal intercourse,' to mention a few, were all described and discussed, some with graphic pictorial demonstrations."

Arthur J. Delaney, "The Grotesque World of Today's Sex Education," *New Oxford Review*, p. 16, May 1996.

"[Having sex with] the male animal, whether it is a dog, horse, bull, or some other species, may provide considerable erotic excitement for the boy or older adult....His enjoyment of the relationship is enhanced by the fact that the male animal responds to the point of orgasm....Psychically, animal relations may become of considerable significance to the boy who is having regular experience...[and] in no point basically different from those that are involved in erotic responses to human situations."

Wardell Pomeroy: Co-author of the Kinsey Reports; *Boys and Sex*, In Judith A. Reisman, *KINSEY: Crimes & Consequences*, p.115. 1998.

pursuit of ever greater sexual excitement through experimentation with novel sexual behaviors. Since the nature of addiction is to demand higher and higher levels of participation by the addict, and since the quality of novelty eventually wears off, we can see in sexual addiction a built-in motivation to pursue ever more frequent, bizarre and aberrant behaviors. Many of these behaviors would be shock or shame-producing for the addict, thus increasing the emotional "jolt" as required by the escalating demands of addiction. The homosexual lifestyle fits easily into this description; it is a powerful addictive pattern, characterized by frequent, bizarre and intense forms of sexual gratification.

Moral Drift

If such a model accurately represents the progressive nature of sexual addiction and explains how some people become deeply enmeshed in the "gay" lifestyle, it can also be extrapolated to our society. The desire for sexual *excitement* is a normal impulse in human beings; on the other hand, what constitutes sexual adventure is relative to a person's prior sexual experience and to his own moral limits and those of his society. For example, sexual adventure for the average American in the 1950s was undoubtedly far less exotic than what probably constitutes sexual adventure for the average person today.

It stands to reason that the more society normalizes sexual deviance, the more the average person will tend to view deviant behavior as an option. Further, the more common a sexually deviant behavior becomes, the less it will tend to satisfy the more sexually adventurous members of society, a group which now includes young people. What occurs then is a society-wide search for stronger stimuli, an inevitable self-perpetuating moral drift by society across the continuum of sexual deviance. This process accelerates as society cuts its moorings to the traditional heterosexual norm.

Most of the arguments against sexual deviance and for the heterosexual norm relate to society's need to protect marriage and the family. The institutionalization of sexual adventure within a

CALL IT ANYTHING BUT "GAY"

"There's a coarseness, a deadening coarseness, in the experience of most homosexuals. The experiences are quick, and hard, and brutal, and the pattern of them is practically unchanging. Their act of love is like the jabbing of a hypodermic needle to which they're addicted but which is more and more empty of real interest and surprise."

Tennessee Williams, from the play, *Confessional*, in Charles Socarides, M.D., *Homosexuality: A Freedom Too Far, p. 125. 1995.*

"Homosexual sexuality is perverse and unhealthy, both physically and emotionally. We put on such a respectable image, but inside we were miserable and ashamed. Like many young gays I tried to commit suicide because I didn't think there was a way out."

Richard "Jonah" Weller, Handbill, "The Voice They Want Silenced: A former homosexual man speaks out about homosexuality and the politics of dishonesty," 1992.

"Not everyone is happy and proud of their choice to live the 'gay' life!....[I am one of] thousands of people who, after experiencing the homosexual life, are disillusioned, 'used up,' left broken and injured, or just plain lonely and hungering for love — for true meaningful family relationships."

D.L. "Sonny" Weaver, "Finding Freedom From the Not-So-Gay Life-Choice," p. 1, 1992.

society, accompanied by many forms of sexual behavior which degrade the individual and work against the principles of committed, selfless, loving family relationships, is a deathblow to that society's cohesion and health.

"Gay" Behavior

We will not take the opportunity, in this book, to discuss the details of "gay" sex practices. Frankly, we believe it is emotionally stressful to read descriptions of the behaviors which are routinely practiced in much of the "gay" community. It will suffice to point out that many practices which are considered normal among homosexuals do not fall inside the range of behaviors which an average person would consider acceptable, even under the heading of sexual adventure. Consequently, the concept of sexual adventure in the "gay" community lies at the extreme end of the range of sexual deviance. Many homosexuals at the fringes of the "gay" community practice forms of perversion which most people do not even know exist (and can be thankful that they don't). We have provided a list of resources at the end of this book for parents who wish (even after this warning) to learn more about what could await their child should he or she be recruited into the "gay" lifestyle, or fall into some other form of sexual addiction.

"Gay" Misery

In defense of the assertion that homosexuality is a condition over which one has no control, homosexual activists often state that no-one would *choose* to be "gay." They strongly imply that if they themselves had had a choice, they would *not* have chosen to be homosexual. In other words, they tacitly admit that the homosexual lifestyle is not "gay," but miserable. Some have laid the blame for homosexuals' unhappiness (and the high rates of suicide, domestic violence, and drug and alcohol addiction in the "gay" community) upon society. They argue that society's disapproval of homosexuality is what causes pain in the lives of homosexuals, that

"DATA TORTURE" HIDES "GAY" GUILT

"The oft stated claim by militant gays that they are statistically no more likely to engage in pederasty than heterosexuals has no empirical basis. A 1985 study of arrests in 12 U.S. jurisdictions showed, on average, about 40 percent of arrests for pederastic homosexuals. Another recent study, touted by gays as evidence to support their claim of being no more likely than heteros to engage in such behavior, actually proved the exact opposite. The study was done by a team of researchers from the University of Colorado who, according to the leader, Dr. Carole Jenny, set out to prove that homosexuals were not more likely to molest children....In any case, the researchers looked at 269 cases at a child-molestation clinic and found that 50 cases, or 18.5 percent, were male-on-male molestation. Since homosexuals make up probably less than 5 percent of the population [the actual figure is about 2%], this would seem to indicate a disproportionate molestation rate. So the investigators engaged in what is known in the scientific community as 'data torture.' *Without interviewing the molesters*, the interviewers decided that most of those offenders who engaged in homosexual sex weren't really homosexuals. Only one of the 50 actually qualified as gay once the data had gotten the full S&M treatment. The sudy was then touted as evidence that gays don't molest children."

Paul Mulshine, "Man-Boy Love," *Heterodoxy,* p.11, September 1994 (emphasis ours).

the only solution to "gay" misery is for society to accept and affirm the homosexual lifestyle. Such a claim is less believable in light of the fact that many of the activists who make it, live and work in overwhelmingly "gay"-affirming communities. The best response to such an argument, however, comes from the ex-"gay" community. Men and women who have left the homosexual lifestyle report that their lives are happy and improved. These former "gays," many of whom now enjoy the pleasures and rewards of heterosexual marriage and child-rearing, offer themselves as living proof that homosexuals can change. Many ex-"gays" also warn that societal affirmation of the homosexual lifestyle hurts "gays" who *want* to fight to overcome their sexual addiction — by removing one of their strongest motivations to succeed: social disapproval of "gay" behavior (not to mention that such affirmation may actively discourage homosexuals from seeking help).

A logical explanation for the unhappiness which characterizes the homosexual lifestyle is that homosexuals are aware, at some level, that their behavior is physically and emotionally destructive. Rates of sexually transmitted disease, for example, are astronomically high in the "gay" community (especially among men) leading to a drastically reduced lifespan for both male and female homosexuals (an average life expectancy of 39 for males, 52 for females). And who can say what degree of psychological harm results from rejecting one's self-evident heterosexual design and engaging in behaviors that violate the obvious natural purpose and function of human sexuality? The subconscious mind acts as a powerful force in shaping one's emotions. No amount of self-deception or affirmation by others will make a person truly happy with his lifestyle if, subconsciously, he remains aware that his behavior is abnormal and harmful.

Sex with Children

Certainly not every homosexual is a pedophile as well, but many people who engage in homosexual behavior also pursue sexual relationships with children and youths. When confronted

"Although homosexuals are less than three percent of the population of the United States, one-third of all child molestation cases involve homosexual activity."

Psychological Reports, vol. 58, pp. 327-337, 1986.

"Boys who are molested often find that telling others that someone took control of them is an extremely difficult thing to admit because it isn't 'manly' to allow such things to happen. Conversely, in some situations, if a girl is molested, it is not as threatening for them to disclose. For example, in a case in southern California, a man was involved sexually with and photographed approximately 150 boys between the ages of 6 and 14 years....He was discovered only after he took pictures of some girls who told their parents afterward."

Seth L. Goldstein, *The Sexual Exploitation of Children: A Practical Guide to Assessment, Investigation, and Intervention*, p. 33, 1987.

with this fact, spokesmen for the "gay" movement typically retort that "ninety-eight percent of child molestations are committed by heterosexual men." This statistic is a mainstay of "gay" rhetoric and is misleading for several reasons. As in the presentations of Alfred Kinsey, both the definitions and the criteria for classifying are closely controlled to favor a "gay"-positive result. The ninety-eight percent statistic is reached by a system of categorizing offenders by whether they identify *themselves* as heterosexual or homosexual, not by simply looking at the gender of the child and of the offender. Thus, a man who sexually molests a twelve-year-old boy is categorized as a *heterosexual* molester if the man is married or identifies himself as *primarily* heterosexual. In other words, the statistic is based on the assumptions of sexual orientation theory and not on the homosexual or heterosexual nature of the acts themselves. Such a process makes the statistic utterly meaningless as to the question of whether people who engage in homosexual behavior are more likely to molest or seduce children. Even if the assumptions of sexual orientation theory were true, a system which categorized offenders by sexual orientation based upon self-reporting could not be considered reliable. It is reasonable to believe that offenders with a homosexual "orientation" would tend to identify themselves as heterosexual simply to make themselves appear more normal to the authorities.

When they have used a behavioral definition of homosexuality, various studies have found that from twenty-five to forty percent of child molestations involved homosexual conduct. This statistic, when combined with the fact that homosexuals represent no more than two percent of the population, indicates a much higher per capita rate of pedophilic behavior in the "gay" community than occurs in society as a whole.

Adult/Child "Consensual" Sex

Another definitional problem in any discussion about sexual activity between adults and young people is the question of "consensual" sex. Most parents would say that, by definition, a

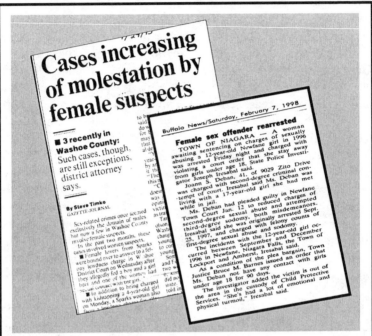

Cases increasing of molestation by female suspects

■ 3 recently in Washoe County: Such cases, though, are still exceptions, district attorney says.

By Steve Timko
GAZETTE-JOURNAL

Sex-related crimes once seemed exclusively the domain of males but now a few in Washoe County involve female suspects.

In the past two months, these cases involved women suspects.

■ Female lovers from Sparks were bound over to answer to a felony lewdness charge in Washoe District Court on Wednesday after they allegedly fed a boy and a girl beer and one of the women had sex and contact with the girl.

■ In addition to being charged with kidnapping a 4-year-old girl on Monday, a Sparks woman also

Buffalo News/Saturday, February 7, 1998

Female sex offender rearrested

TOWN OF NIAGARA — A woman awaiting sentencing on charges of sexually abusing a 12-year-old girl in 1996 was arrested Friday night and charged with violating a court order that she stay away from Joseph Iresabal, 41, of 9029 Zito Drive, gator Joseph Iresabal, 41, of 9029 Zito Drive, State Police Investigator Joann S. Deban, said.

Joann S. Deban, charged with second-degree criminal contempt of court. Iresabal said Ms. Deban was living with a 17-year-old girl she had met while in jail.

Ms. Deban had pleaded guilty in Newfane Town Court Jan. 12 to reduced charges of second-degree sexual abuse and attempted third-degree sodomy, both misdemeanors. Iresabal said she was originally arrested Sept. 25, 1997, and charged with felony counts of first-degree sexual abuse and sodomy.

The incidents with the 12-year-old girl occurred between September and December 1996 in Newfane, Niagara Falls, the Town of Lockport and Amherst, Iresabal said.

As a condition of the plea bargain, Town Justice Bruce M. Barnes issued an order that Ms. Deban not have any contact with girls under age 18 for 90 days.

The investigator added the victim is out of the area in the custody of Child Protective Services. "She's had a lot of emotional and physical turmoil," Iresabal said.

"In 1973 a guide entitled *Where the Young Ones Are* was published in the United States, giving the male tourist information about the availability of child prostitutes in that country...In the late 1970s and 1980s the *Spartacus* Gay Guides, published in the Netherlands, provided male homosexual tourists with up-to-date advice about the availability of sexual contacts in most countries. They publish specific advice about where to stay, where boys are available, how to make contact and how much to pay, as well as giving advice about the legal situation for homosexuals."

Judith Ennew, *The Sexual Exploitation of Children*, p.106, 1986.

child cannot "consent" to sexual relations with an adult, yet their children might not agree. Children and teens often do not complain to the authorities about sexual encounters, even forcible ones, they may have had with adults or older teens. Parents in Philadelphia were shocked several years ago when a predator who called himself "Fast Eddie" announced that he had AIDS, and, out of concern for his sexual partners, disclosed that he had seduced over two hundred boys in the area. What is significant in this story is that *none* of these boys had ever turned him in as a molester. They probably viewed themselves as free moral agents capable of consenting to sex with an adult. The real question is, how many "Fast Eddies" are prowling America's cities today, and how many of their juvenile victims never make the statistics? The fact is that homosexual pedophiles have always played a central role in the "gay" movement.

Rhetoric Can't Hide the "Gay" Focus on Youth

One of the original planks in the 1972 "gay rights" agenda (one which has never been renounced) is a call for the repeal of age-of-consent laws for children. The only openly pederastic (remember that pederasty is man-boy sex) organizations in the United States are run by and for homosexual men. Harry Hay, founder of the first major homosexual organization in the United States, the Mattachine Society, and an icon of the American "gay" movement, actively supports one of these organizations, the North American Man-Boy Love Association (NAMBLA). Mainstream "gay" travel books advise homosexual men on how to procure boys for sex in foreign countries. Lesbian-oriented literature commonly describes scenes of adult women having sex with young girls. In recent years the "gay" movement has tried to publicly distance itself from advocates of adult-child sex, but homosexual pedophiles are as prominent as ever in the "gay" community and, thanks to the society-wide campaign of "gay" recruitment, more *active* than ever in seducing boys and girls into the "gay" lifestyle.

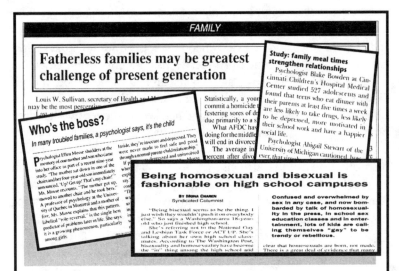

"Young parents....have to be good role models -- moms and dads who really love one another, and show it, with a lot of hugs and kisses. They shouldn't spare the hugs and kisses for their children either. When little girls are about three years old, I'd advise their fathers to present them with a special present, preferably a doll, something that will assure the little girl of her femininity. Fathers who demonstrate approval and admiration of their daughters in this fashion are helping to set the course for a normal feminine development. In my practice, I have found that lesbians had deep feelings of inferiority as little girls. Anything that parents can do to make their kids feel proud of their identity -- as young men, as young women -- will help the process."

Charles W. Socarides, M.D., *Homosexuality -- A Freedom Too Far*, p. 279, 1995.

Step Four

STRENGTHEN YOUR FAMILY

We have looked at the reasons why parents should be concerned about "gay" recruitment and the homosexual agenda. We now turn to the question of how to recruit-proof a child. The first key is a strong family.

What Makes a Family?

Earlier we rejected the notion put forth by "gay" activists that "love makes a family." Such a concept might appeal to the soft and sentimental side of our personalities, but intellectually we know that love alone cannot make a family. A family is more substantial than that; it is the social unit upon which all of civilization is built. But what does family structure itself have to do with our definition of family? Why can't just any set of unrelated individuals live together as a "family," simply by calling themselves one?

To understand the answers to these questions, we must look deeper into the way that people are organized and functionally related in families. All families, as defined in every society, begin with a male-female pair (this is true even in our age of artificial

THE "GAY" FAMILY

"While incest is generally viewed as dysfunctional for the family - and this is true of heterosex incest - I will argue that at origin, homosex incest plays a functional role in the development of the family."

Lesbian activist and first female president of the Gay and Lesbian Press Association (GLPA), Susan Cavin, *Lesbian Origins*, p. 57, 1989.

"In order to raise children with equality, we must take them away from families and communally raise them."

Dr. Mary Jo Bane, Feminist and Asst. Professor of Education, Wellesley College.

"I love Wayne very much, and I never confuse that love with the sexual pleasure I might enjoy with someone else. . . Meanwhile, Wayne and I have been discussing the possibility of adding a third person to our relationship . . . ."

Mark Pendleton, "Married . . .But Not Dead," Frontiers magazine, March *16, 1993, p. 29.* quoted in *Lambda Report,* Spring 1994.

"The cheating ratio of 'married' [committed] gay males, given enough time, approaches 100%."

Marshall Kirk and Hunter Madsen, *After the Ball*, p. 330, 1990.

insemination and surrogate parenting). Just as this pair contains within it the reproductive possibility of many offspring, even many generations, so also it contains the seeds of the society and culture to which these offspring will belong. This is so because we humans are social beings who learn through our childhood experiences in our families how to interact in complex, organized, purposeful and even ingenious and selfless ways. In addition, at least in our "Western" cultural tradition, we humans produce *individuals*, people who regard themselves as whole and independent beings, beings with rights and responsibilities which derive from their individual worth and autonomy. Both the social being and the individual spring from the possibilities contained in the male-female pair, but these conflicting entities are only effectively balanced in a child's life in the context of an intact, healthy family structure.

The Heterosexual Duality

The meaning held in the male-female pair begins with the lesson of duality. The central idea of relationship is self and other, "you" and "I." This idea forms early in a child's mind as he or she differentiates "self" from "mother," but it is very incomplete. The child needs to understand the far-reaching implications of being equal to, yet unlike, another human, and of having to step outside the limits of one's own personality and experience to understand the motivations of another.

The mother and father represent the two poles of humanity to their child, who can see that they don't look the same, sound the same, or even move or react in the same ways. Nevertheless, they clearly love each other and their child, and this circumstance of both love and obligation leads them to interact in many ways which do not escape the attention of the child. The child sees them having conflicts of self-interest and clashes of personality; he then sees them each set aside some part of their personal claims to reach a resolution. The child sees them approach a common goal from completely different, distinctly male and female perspectives; he sees them cooperate, each contributing differently, to reach the goal.

WOMEN'S FUNCTION TO "CIVILIZE" MEN

"The crucial process of civilization is the subordination of male sexual impulses and biology to the long-term horizons of female sexuality. The overall sexual behavior of women in the modern world differs relatively little from the sexual life of women in primitive societies. It is male behavior which must be changed to create a civilized order. Men lust, but they know not what for; they wander, and lose track of the goal; they fight and compete, but they forget the prize; they spread seed, but spurn the seasons of growth; they chase power and glory, but miss the meaning of life. In creating civilization, women transform male lust into love; channel male wanderlust into jobs, homes, and families; link men to specific children; rear children into citizens; change hunters into fathers; divert male will to power into a drive to create. Women conceive the future that men tend to flee, they feed the children that men ignore."

"...The woman's place is in the home, and she does her best when she can get the man there too, inducing him to submit most human activity to the domestic values of civilization....The fact is that there is no way that women can escape their supreme responsibilities in civilized society without endangering civilization itself."

George Gilder, *Men and Marriage*, p. 1, 176-177, 1995.

The child sees when they fail to understand each other and struggle to communicate, each slowly reaching a better working knowledge of the other. The child sees them show delight in each other's differences, in ways which reveal their natural complementarity and which model their unique qualities of maleness and femaleness. He see them behave sometimes as if they were one person, other times as complete opposites. He sees all this daily, in an intimate way, set against a background of many events and stages of his life. And he never fails to absorb the smallest detail because so much of it centers on him.

The Root of Civilization

On this central core of the mother-father relationship are constructed the functions of the family: nurturing, accountability, intimacy, protection, training in every aspect of social behavior, skills development, recreation, comfort, advocacy, companionship, and many more. And the values and practices which support these functions are also modeled by the parent couple: altruism, compassion, loyalty, trustworthiness, courage, forgiveness, respect, considerateness, cheerfulness, willingness and many more. In short, the family is there to meet most of the needs of all of its members, and all of this complex functioning is passed from generation to generation by an originating pair, a man and a woman who commit themselves to this task.

Overcoming Family Dysfunction

A few decades ago, it would not have been necessary to describe how a family is built and what it is supposed to do. Then, as now, many families did not match this "ideal" of family function, but nearly everyone agreed on the model. Then, as now, there were many variations on the central pattern: members were lost or gained, generations lived together, sibling families shared parental duties among themselves. Then, as now, functional success was a relative thing; some families functioned well in many areas, some failed to

CAN LOVE ALONE MAKE A FAMILY?

"It is too simplistic to believe that 'love is love.' Few people would say, when a single woman and a married man are attracted to each other, 'Love is love—that's all that matters.' Nor would they say so about the attraction of a teacher for a student, or a pedophile for a child, or a sadomasochist for his partner. As for homosexual love, there are many caring gay relationships—but many psychotherapists believe that gay love is inherently *limited* and *conflictual* because it is rooted in a developmental deficit. It is also inherently problematic because gay relationships are almost never monogamous. One must ask: What can we infer about a type of relationship that gay writers admit 'requires' outside sexual contacts for *survival?*

For thousands of years, civilization has recognized heterosexual marriage as the foundation of society. The new notion that 'love is love' and that a family consists of 'any group of people who happen to love one another" should not be so uncritically accepted—as compassionate and inclusive as these ideas may sound.'

School Sex-Education Guidelines: Teaching About Homosexuality, National Association for Research and Therapy of Homosexuality, p. 5, 1996.

function well in most respects. But common knowledge of the model helped people to correct the flaws. When a family member was lost, for example, through death or desertion or divorce, other people recognized *what functions were missing*, and often succeeded in replacing them. When a family member malfunctioned, through violence or addiction or criminal behavior, responsible relatives often moved in to separate that person from the people who were harmed, and to undo the damage, if possible. There was a common standard, and most people could judge whether or not it was being met, and act accordingly.

We have the same ability today, if we are willing to accept the model, based on a healthy male-female relationship. There is no reason why a single-parent family can't accomplish most of the functions of the "model" family, if the parent knows what those functions are and is willing to find people and means to fulfill them. Grandparents, close family friends, church families, neighbors can often provide what is missing. The important thing is to *know* what is missing and then to work to replace it. The same thing applies to families that are seriously malfunctioning, if one or both parents is willing to acknowledge what's wrong, then repairs can be made and functions can be replaced. Families don't have to be thrown away just because they're broken.

What Is *Not* a Family

While a family can be repaired, one cannot be constructed from unrelated parts. A family is more than simply a collection of exchangeable components. It is not like a machine which can be disassembled and reassembled with no loss of function or serviceability; it is more like a living organism for which replacement parts are always something less than what was lost — like a prosthetic limb to replace a missing arm or leg. Such a substitute may be adequate to meet a person's basic needs, perhaps substituting so well as to be nearly unnoticeable, but it is never equal or preferable to the real thing. For this reason a homosexual "family" is the most inadequate of substitutes for raising a child.

Scores of women are acting as surrogates for gay men

SOCIAL ISSUES: While the number is small, it is increasing, experts on surrogate parents say.

By FRANK BRUNI
The New York Times

BROKEN ARR
Diane Thornton s
when she looked a
and 3-year-old
there was a debt
life, a kindness u
Thornton and
mantic partner,
ans, each concei
boys with sperm
gay friend, and sh
if he ever wante
raise a child him
say 'boo.' "
He never did. S
a social worker w
suburb of Tulsa,
of a surrogacy ag
men among its p
ents. Two months
plus expenses, she
boy, who lives wit
his father's partn
les.
"This child wa
their hearts long
conceived in my
said. "I gave him
added, referring
that ended in a s
ture delivery, "bu
my hopes in him
were doing that."
The price of sur
$30,000 to $70,000
gate's fee and leg
expenses — is
most people.
As uncommon
actions may be
baby for a gay ma
are not singular. I
is still grappling
tudes toward gay
equal rights or
alone raising chi

she said. A cousin's painful experience with infertility had persuaded her to do something to help people frustrated in their desire to have children, and a community college project that involved reading "And the Band Played On," a book about the AIDS epidemic, had filled her

several years in the Navy and is studying to become a high school teacher. "I know how I am with my kids," he said, "and I'd hate to be in the shoes of someone who couldn't have kids."
Thornton, Cohen and Waterman are working with Growing Generations, an agency in Bev-

> "We have just published the largest and most objective study of the effects of homosexual parenting...using official records of child custody battles from across the country. ...Court officials judged that heterosexual parents harmed about 8% of their children, but homosexual parents harmed 78% of their children. Until now, of the 30 or so published studies all but one (by Family Research Institute) have used volunteers" [i.e., the results of the FRI studies have greater reliability].

Dr. Paul Cameron,
Family Research Report
(a publication of the
Family Research
Institute), p. 1,
May-June, 1998.

Not only is the child disadvantaged by the absence of his natural parent of the same or opposite gender, but the proffered replacement (the natural parent's same-sex partner) doesn't fit, like trying to substitute a leg for an arm.

Single-Parent Denial

A final consideration deserves mention in this discussion of the role of family structure in raising healthy children. We must acknowledge that many single parents, for various reasons, cling to the belief that their children are not disadvantaged by the loss of the other parent. Such an attitude may contribute to the possibility of gender dysfunction in a child if it deters a single mom or dad from finding a parental substitute for his or her child to learn from. Popular culture has not helped in this regard, legitimizing as it does the concept of throwaway marriages and "take-it-all-in-stride" kids. Significantly, most former homosexuals testify that family dysfunction and/or missing parental role models played a major part in their becoming "gay." Thankfully, however, the majority of single parents seem to recognize that broken and incomplete homes affect children very deeply and work to provide their children with parental surrogates. (See "Advice to Single Parents" in Step Five).

This having been said, we return to the specific family dynamics which help steer a child towards healthy sexual function as an adult.

Restore Traditional Roles in the Home

If our model of the healthy family is true, the thing to repair first in a dysfunctional home and the relationship to strengthen first in an already healthy home is the husband-wife relationship. We have discussed the ways in which healthy couples interact. Here we focus on the distinct roles of husbands and wives in a family.

A child is better prepared to avoid recruitment into the "gay" lifestyle if his parents model healthy male and female roles in the

LIKE MOTHER, LIKE DAUGHTER

"I have always been open with my daughter about my lesbianism. While I would never try to manipulate her sexually, I am very proud to be the lesbian mother of a lesbian daughter! At age nine she started having sex with other girls with my support and approval. My daugher looks femme, yet acts very butch and is completely secure in her sexuality. Her early experiences were with girls at school, in the neighborhood, on sports teams, etc. Actually, she had a lot of them. Then at age 12 she developed a crush on one of my friends. She told me about her feelings, and I replied directly and emphatically that I approved. Since that time she has mostly dated adult women. Whether we want to admit it or not, there are lesbians who include teenage girls among the types of women they find appealing, sexually and otherwise. As teens, some lesbians had their own loving sexual encounters with adult women. It is hypocritical for them to now deny the same opportunity to contemporary teenage lesbians. To me the ones being controlling and manipulative are those who tell the teens they must not have sex with adult women. Now that is control!"

Monica, Oklahoma City, OK, *Lesbian Connection*, November-December 1997.

home. A child not only needs to see his parents working through their differences to achieve common goals, he needs to envision *himself* as one of the parts of a successful couple. He or she needs to identify what it means to be a man or a woman. When we speak of roles in this context we are not necessarily talking about the division of housework, but about the way in which a husband and wife relate as a man and a woman. Feminist doctrine envisions husbands and wives as the equivalent of partners in a business enterprise in which roles are interchangeable and duties are apportioned according to a partner's greater knowledge or skills. But marriage is *not* a business and many of men's and women's most important roles are *not* interchangeable. While men and women are equal in worth and dignity, they are not equal in traits and qualities which are helpful in meeting various family needs. Each tends to be better at certain things simply by virtue of gender. As violently as some people will react to the suggestion, it remains true that the child with the best chance for developing a healthy gender identity and enjoying happiness in life will have parents that look something like Ozzie and Harriet.

The Father Factor

If a family seeking to protect a child from homosexuality were somehow limited to enhancing just one factor in that child's life, it would most certainly be the influence of a father's love. Of all the factors which shape a child's sense of sexual identity, the influence of a father seems the most vital. Among the published testimonies of former homosexuals, *both male and female*, the parent most often blamed for leaving children emotionally vulnerable to sexual seduction or gender identity problems is Dad. Conversely, the factor which appears to characterize a home which produces sexually healthy offspring is the presence of a loving, involved father during childhood. The mere presence of a father in the home, however, does not ensure a child's healthy sexual identity. Many ex-"gays" report that their fathers were physically present in their families, but were somehow distant or detached from the lives of

FROM HOMEMAKERS TO HOMEWRECKERS

"Being a housewife is an illegitimate profession ...the choice to serve and be protected and plan towards being a family-maker is a choice that shouldn't be. The heart of radical feminism is to change that."

Vivian Gornick, feminist author, University of Illinois, *The Daily Illini*, April 25, 1981.

"Marriage has existed for the benefit of men; and has been a legally sanctioned method of control over women...We must work to destroy it. The end of the institution of marriage is a necessary condition for the liberation of women. Therefore it is important for us to encourage women to leave their husbands and not to live individually with men...All of history must be re-written in terms of oppression of women. We must go back to ancient female religions like witchcraft."

From "The Declaration of Feminism," November 1971.

"The oppression of gay people starts in the most basic unit of society, the family, consisting of the man in charge, a slave as his wife, and their children on whom they force themselves as the ideal models."

From "Gay Liberation Front Manifesto - London," 1971, in Lisa Power, *No Bath But Plenty of Bubbles: An Oral History of the Gay Liberation Front*, p. 316, 1995.

their children. Commonly, Dad was an alcoholic or sometimes just a workaholic.

Often the fathers of "gay" men who adopt an effeminate persona are themselves ultra-macho and aloof from or condemning of their sons. Lesbian sexual dysfunction, as well, seem closely linked to the father's rejection or abuse, traumatizing refusals to love, which result in an unwillingness to trust any man for emotional security or physical intimacy.

Lesbianism and the Destruction of Fatherhood

Since the rise of radical feminism in the 1960s and 70s, the perception of a man's role in the family has changed dramatically. In feminist thought, fathers have been removed from their roles as chief breadwinners and protectors of their wives and children and have become almost superfluous in the family unit.   In lesbian political rhetoric, fathers often appear as society's chiefest villains; they are, by their very nature, presumed to be child abusers and wife beaters.   Lesbianism has become the driving force behind the modern feminist movement (the part of it which gets media attention) and it is the lesbian distortion of feminism with which families must contend in their efforts to recruit-proof their children.

Until recent decades, feminism has been family centered. Early feminists envisioned a society in which women were empowered, not for their own selfish purposes, but to fight injustice and immorality which threatened their families and their society. Only since the "gay" movement has become a more potent political force has feminism come to be dominated by lesbians and female homosexualists. The feminist agenda has shifted from altruistic and egalitarian goals to more selfish ones, including the goal of consequence-free sexual liberty.   Traditional feminism has not viewed men as adversaries to be defeated, but as family members to be persuaded. The lesbian-influenced version, however, portrays men as enemies of women whose role can be sidestepped. The two most feminine of all roles, those of wife and mother, are treated as evidence of patriarchal oppression.   The hallmark attitudes of

THE PRO-FAMILY ROOTS OF FEMINISM

"'Purity' is a term borrowed from the second half of the 19th century, when women strove to restore to America the social virtue and purity which was lost as a result of the change from an agrarian to an industrial economy. With the displacement of families to large, impersonal and transient urban areas, the old moral and social order was crumbling. Women of a hundred years ago understood this breakdown threatened their vital, preeminent position, their homes and families. The threat was great and so obvious that it integrated women, both religionists and social feminists alike, into the 'Purity Movement' as they harkened back to the founding moral principles of the nation for the sake of future generations.

The backbone of the purity movement was the Women's Christian Temperance Union and the General Federation of Women's Clubs. Joined by organizations and individuals with a wide array of interests...all made common cause to support women and children by strengthening the family. This coalition of virtuous women saw the social evils of their day: Black Slavery, the White Slave Trade, drug use and alcoholism, prostitution, sexual immorality, child labor, unhealthy diet, lack of respect for women, obscene and impure books, bad hygiene -- as detrimental to women, families and especially to children. Agreeing upon the moral foundations of America these women changed laws and public policies for the betterment of society, responding to the call to virtue in their times."

Judith Reisman, PhD, *RSVP America*, p.1-3, 1996

radical feminism clearly did not originate among emotionally healthy women, but they are entirely consistent with the emotional profile which often characterizes lesbians: bitterness and anger toward men and their roles. Many women have tolerated the more extreme distortions of feminism because they were sold as part of a larger package of beliefs and goals which held genuine appeal for women: greater economic independence and career opportunities, workplace equality, and greater recognition for their personal and collective accomplishments outside of the domestic sphere.

Lesbianized feminism today serves the "gay" agenda far better than it serves women. Indeed, the goals and strategies of the "gay" agenda have been recast as tenets of feminism which, especially at universities, have been marketed to women as personal goals to be zealously pursued. Where else but in the upside-down world of homosexuality would femininity be redefined in masculine terms (competitive, aggressive, and individualistic) and feminist goals be stretched to include the "right" to kill on the battlefield? Where else but in the "gay"-influenced mind would childbearing be seen as an obstacle to the "more important" benefits, sexual freedom and pleasure — benefits which are held to easily outweigh the value of an unborn child's life? What other group but the "gay" community would place a higher value on encouraging women to put self before family than on exhorting men to put family before self? (Recall that making men more responsible, not enabling women to be less responsible, was the goal of the early women's movement.)

Who Really Benefits from "Gender" Feminism?

As with any other social movement which threatens the traditional family, we must ask who truly benefits from radical, lesbianized feminism (often called "gender feminism"). The average woman does not, certainly. Under modern feminism, earlier victories have been turned against women. The hard-won option of choosing a career over family, for example, has now become a mandate to have both; women are made to feel that they haven't lived up to their full potential if they stay at home to raise

LESBIAN FEMINISM

"'Any woman can be a lesbian,' says the song. 'Feminism is the theory, lesbianism is the practice,' goes the slogan. And to many women, the 'women's community' is a lesbian community."

Beth Elliot, "Bisexuality, the best thing that ever happened to lesbian-feminism?," in *Bi Any Other Name: Bisexual People Speak Out*, Loraine Hutchins and Kaahumanu (eds.), p. 324, 1991.

A FATHER'S INFLUENCE

"Victims of the 'gay agenda' have many things in common from childhood. An absentee father, (lack of masculine influence), a dad that was abusive towards him or his mother, the role model that abuses alcohol or drugs, or has a sexual problem himself (such as an addiction to pornography), or a stepfather that they disliked. Also, there are the many who had a domineering mother, and a passive father...Homosexuals are attracted to boys, but have no luck with a young man who has a close and intimate relationship with Dad."

Richard "Jonah" Weller, handbill, "Honesty Set Me Free!," 1997.

their children. But the "gay" movement does benefit, and substantially, from the indoctrination of women with radical feminist goals. The devaluing of the pivotal role in the family, the at-home wife and mother, helps to destabilize the family itself. The undermined and downgraded image of family life, added to the many poorly-functioning families, makes the normalizing of "alternative" lifestyles such as homosexuality easier, and the contrast between normalcy and deviancy less noticeable.

"Gender" feminism also encourages women to seek so-called equality in some of the least healthy areas of male behavior, such as sexual libertinism. The increase of sexually libertine behavior and attitudes among members of both sexes has caused major disruptions in the institutions of marriage and the family, as well as unleashing on society epidemics of sexually transmitted disease, illegitimate births, abortions, infanticides and violent behavior associated with sexual addiction. It has also increased the incidence of divorce and "serial marriage" and has made men less willing to accept the responsibility of marriage and fatherhood.

The Disappearing Dad

Perhaps lesbian-dominated feminism's most telling blow to the traditional family is the emasculation of fathers. Stripped of authority as the heads of their households and robbed of the sense of worth and purpose which men derive from their traditional roles, fathers in feminist-influenced homes often lose sight of their importance to their wives and children. Such men may then seek their sense of self-worth and value outside of the family — in their careers or perhaps even in extramarital relationships. The vital role of the father is weakened and diminished, or lost altogether, resulting in ever greater numbers of "fatherless" children. These children will be willing to believe whatever radical feminism teaches about the "evils" of family and fatherhood; conversely, they will also be doubly vulnerable to the "fatherly" approach of adult sexual predators.

GENDER ROLES MATTER

"To the sexual liberal, gender is a cage. Behind cruel bars of tradition, men and women for centuries have looked longingly across forbidden spaces at one another and yearned to be free of sexual roles."

George Gilder, *Men and Marriage*, p. 115, 1995.

"Every society recognizes a particular emotional difference between men and women...the male strength and dominance, and the female gentleness and endurance portrayed in our novels and movies mirror not merely *our* society's view of the emotional natures of men and women, but the views of every society that has ever existed..."

Steven Goldberg, *Ph.D., Why Men Rule: A Theory of Male Dominance*, p. 3. 1993.

"I don't know where this idea came from, but the voguish practice of encouraging little boys to play with dolls is a stupid and dangerous one. Boys normally learn sensitivity from their sisters. Or from their little girl playmates, or, later, from their classmates in school. They don't need dolls. What they need most, these days, is a sense of identity as little men, destined to become fathers, like their dads."

Charles W. Socarides, M.D., *Homosexuality- A Freedom Too Far*, p. 279, 1995.

Androgynous Children

A final area in which "gender" feminism has influenced the family is the sex roles of children. Starting in the 1960s, certain child care manuals advocated encouraging children to take opposite-gender roles in their play, i.e., trying to get boys to play with dolls or girls to focus on trucks. Certainly, under normal circumstances, no child should be discouraged from playing with the toys he or she chooses, but to try to *change* these choices in favor of opposite-gender ones sends confusing messages, suggesting to the child that there is something wrong with his or her gender. Recent years have seen a retreat from this kind of foolishness, even as popular journalism has rediscovered the importance of sexual differences. But the bitter heritage of "gender" feminism is still with us, and goes on contributing to the erosion of the family.

Parents of both sexes should examine their beliefs and assumptions about the roles of men and women, and test whether these views contribute or detract from unity and cooperation in their family and marriage. If a belief or practice only promotes selfishness or conflict between the sexes, then your family would be better off without it.

Build Healthy Character Qualities In Your Child

Your effort to recruit-proof your child should include teaching him basic attitudes that we might call strength of character. Unfortunately, along with the decline in morality in our culture, we have seen a tendency in many parents to indulge children's weaknesses, perhaps because parents have been more inclined to indulge themselves. All children naturally develop some level of self-restraint and personal responsibility in childhood, but the strength of such qualities in a child's character are largely determined by parents. Parents who (as a team) firmly, consistently and lovingly *insist* on proper behavior, good habits, and a positive attitude will be more likely to produce strong and emotionally secure children; children who will be less vulnerable to "gay"

PRE-KINSEYAN PRINCIPLES OF HEALTHY LOVE, MARRIAGE & FAMILY LIFE

1. The responsibility for human sexuality instruction lies with the parents. It should be taught as a component of marriage and family life....

3. Values mean right conduct, chastity, and obeying an authority higher than personal urges and selfish-indulgence.

4. Abstinence before marriage is for emotional and physical health....

5. For healthy psychological and physical development, chastity is a moral dimension and needs to be reinstated as moral virtue.

6. Self-discipline is even more essential in the sexual realm than it is in the areas of work and study.

7. Modesty must be encouraged and elevated....

9. Parent involvement in marriage preparation (not sex) curriculum development is indispensable.

14. Permanent, faithful marriage is the only healthy context for expressing genital sex and creating a healthy environment for children.

Judith Reisman, PhD., *R.S.V.P. America*, pp. 32-33, 1996.

recruitment. Most harmful to a child is a parental figure who confuses indulgence with love and allows the child to define his own rules. Such a child will be forced to learn self-control and other necessary qualities (if he ever learns them) through painful lessons in the real world. Our jails are filled to overflowing with people who haven't yet learned these lessons. So is the "gay" community.

Teach Logic over Emotion

The truth will set you free (but your feelings can mislead you)

One of the most important concepts a parent can teach a child is the value of logical thinking. Logic helps a child to challenge and to test new ideas, preventing him from simply being swept along by his emotions. Unfortunately, the trend in our culture is for people to let themselves be ruled by their feelings and not by logic. Axioms such as "Follow your heart," and "Do what feels right" have, in popular speech, replaced earlier standards like "Use your head." This is partly because of laziness. Reasoning one's way to a logical conclusion can be hard work, but making a decision based on feelings is easy: you determine your emotional response to an idea, then you act upon it. But, as always happens when you follow the line of least effort, there is a problem: over-reliance on feelings can easily cloud a person's reason, allowing him to reach false and sometimes harmful conclusions on important issues. For example, we have seen that pro-"gay" propaganda is intellectually very shallow, yet many non-homosexuals are passionate defenders of the "gay" lifestyle. For many such defenders, whose ranks include a great many young people, the sole explanation for their pro-"gay" stance is their susceptibility to emotional manipulation. They have bought into the notion that "gays" are helpless victims, or confused "gays" with racial groups who are genuinely disadvantaged, and because of their reaction to these issues, preexisting emotions take over. Unfortunately, factual arguments have little impact on feelings-reliant people, so it is very difficult to persuade them of the truth once they have made an emotional commitment to a position.

THE 'FEELINGS' TRAP

"There is no right or wrong way boys or girls should act, and sex by itself never hurt anyone. The only rules we need are simple: *do what feels right to you*, and take care not to hurt anyone else. That way, maybe we can all be comfortable with being the best thing of all -- ourselves."

Don Romesburg, (ed.), *Young, Gay, and Proud!*, 1995.

"The systematic undermining of morality that used to be called 'values clarification' is still going on in our public schools under other labels, now that parents and critics have caught on to what 'values clarification' really means. It means reducing moral principles to mere subjective feelings. The 'non-judgmental' nature of much of the classroom social engineering that goes on is consistent with this emphasis on feelings, on diaries and on other devices that put personal feelings on the same plane as tested knowledge and tested moral principles that enable a society to function."

Thomas Sowell, "Tenured dumbness permeates our schools," column, *Orange County Register*, July, 1998.

This is one reason why parents should stress logical thinking from the very beginning of their child's learning process. And, of course, there is no area of life in which the ability to think logically doesn't give you an advantage.

How to Teach Logic

Logical thinking is taught by example. A parent who establishes sensible rules and applies them fairly and consistently, and who takes time to sit down with a child and think through a problem, will have a pretty good chance of raising a logical and clear-thinking child. A parent whose rules are arbitrary or unreasonable, or who fails to properly enforce or apply the rules, or who deals with personal problems in an emotional and unreasoning way, will probably raise an illogical and emotionally vulnerable child. The principles of teaching logic to a child are much like the principles of bringing about justice in society. Justice requires the equal application of the law; law that is made up of the minimum of rules and restrictions that are necessary to preserve the good order of society. These cannot be arbitrary laws, they must directly serve the best interests of the people and they must be applied fairly to everyone. They must also be firmly and consistently enforced. A truly just society is stable and secure because its citizens know that their system is fair and predictable. In the same manner, a family with a sensible parent, presiding over sensible parenting rules, is a safe and secure environment for children. In the process of growing up in such a home, a child learns the relationship between rational thinking and successful living and is thus less susceptible to emotional manipulation.

De-Sexualize Your Child's Environment

A slogan of "gay" pedophiles which was common in the 1960s is, "Sex before eight, or it's too late." This slogan reflects a belief among pederasts that children are easier targets for later recruitment into the homosexual lifestyle if they are sexualized (molested or

HOW TO PROTECT YOUR CHILD
FROM MOLESTATION

1. Give your youngster clear warnings that no one - not even people in authority - should touch him or her in intimate ways.

2. Insist that schools, camps and other organizations do thorough background checks on anyone who will be working with your child.

3. If your child has negative feelings about a teacher or some other authority figure, explore why the child feels this way.

4. Learn to recognize the signs that a child may have been assaulted; these include chronic unexplained physical complaints, loss of appetite, disturbed sleep, mood change and sudden sexually focused behavior.

5. Believe your child if he says he's been assaulted. Children seldom lie about molestation.

From *Reader's Digest*, "Children for Sale: Pornography's Dark New World," p. 55, July, 1983.

otherwise sexually traumatized) in early childhood. This doesn't mean that older children or teenagers who have never been molested cannot be recruited into homosexuality, just that early sexualization makes children more vulnerable. Alfred Kinsey made the sexualization of children all the more possible by popularizing the view that children are naturally sexual from birth. We forcefully reject such a concept as the wishful and self-justificatory thinking of a man who is arguably the most destructive sexual predator in American history. However, we believe that children can *become* sexualized at any age through sexual trauma. Based upon personal observation, we believe that every person has a built-in "switch" that controls sexual awareness and response. Undisturbed, this switch is probably triggered by the body's hormones during puberty, but premature and traumatic exposure to a sexual experience can also awaken sexual awareness in a child. We believe that such an occurrence is also irreversible; one cannot "unring" the bell.

Wolves Among the Lambs

If our theory in the section above is true, then it should serve as an increased motivation to parents to shield their prepubescent children from premature exposure to sexuality. How can this be accomplished? In a later chapter we will address the impact of sexual imagery and content in entertainment media, but here we will focus on the actual physical contacts your child may have with family members and other children and adults. The first rule is *never, never* trust your child alone with *anyone* who has *ever* been charged or convicted of a sex-related crime involving children, or who you personally know or have good reason to suspect has engaged in such activity (even activity you might consider "minor"). It doesn't matter how much time has passed since the offense or how much counseling the person has received or how hurt he or she will feel by your stance. The nature of this type of sexual compulsion makes such a person absolutely untrustworthy. Sexual obsession with children is a lifelong, insoluble problem for most pedophiles.

"PLAYING HOUSE"

"A growing number of children are molesting other children. These child-aged molesters are influenced by a variety of factors including "night visitors" to their unmarried mother, sexually explicit TV and movies, and school sex education. The strongest influence, however, may be incest and/or being molested by another, usually older, child...*These investigations point up the strong likelihood that children who become prematurely sexual will engage in homosexuality.* Any school or advertising program that teaches kids about sex runs the risk of 'stimulating' youngsters into sexual activity."

Dr. Paul Cameron, *Family Research Report*, March-April 1994. (Emphasis ours.)

"Interviews conducted by police investigators with pedophiles themselves also reveal some startling information. A 52-year-old man told an investigator of 5,000 children he had molested in his lifetime; a 42-year-old Connecticut man told of more than 1,000 children he had molested; and a 62-year-old man, an oil executive with a $11,000-a-month trust fund, admitted to molesting a 'boy a day' for 30 years."

Seth L. Goldstein, *The Sexual Exploitation of Children*, p. 33, 1987.

The Wolf in Lamb's Clothing

Add to the list of people not to trust alone with your child, any other child who appears prematurely sexualized. Such children are not always readily identified, but if a child displays an interest in sexual matters well beyond his age level, he should not be trusted alone with your child. Chances are such a child has already begun exploring his sexual possibilities and will want to share his discoveries with your child. Don't let your less protective friends minimize such activity as harmless games. Childhood sexualization spreads through a community of children like a game of tag, stealing the innocence of every child who is touched. We don't place sexual experimentation by children in the same category with sexual molestation by an adult, which can cause immediate and far more serious emotional problems, but we believe such experimentation does make a child more vulnerable to sexual predators. It is also true that many of the children of today have been sexualized traumatically, either by a predatory adult or teenager, or by exposure to pornography or the like. These children will be likely to pass their distorted and unhealthy attitude about sex on to your child.

Thinking About the Unthinkable

In the event that a parent learns of a problem after the fact, his response should be measured according to the type of activity that has sexualized his child. Molestation by an adult should be reported immediately to the authorities, preferably with the assistance of an advocate for the family such as a lawyer, minister or family counselor, to minimize the traumatic impact on the family. Many parents, out of ignorance of the effect of sexual molestation or fear of the stigma which may attach to the child, choose to sweep the problem under the rug and pretend that nothing has happened. Not only does such a failure to respond allow the sexual predator to preserve his anonymity and his access to other children, but it leaves a ticking time bomb of emotional rage and pain within the abused child. A sexually abused child needs special help to repair the

SAVE SEX, NOT SAFE SEX, SHOULD BE PARENTS' MOTTO

"It is irresponsible for a school counseling program to give the implicit message that abstinence is too dear a price to pay. Children are unlikely to resist their natural sexual inclinations, unless they have *clear expectations from adults that they will do so.*"

School Sex-Education Guidelines: Teaching About Homosexuality, NARTH publication, 1996.

"Premarital sex, particularly with many partners, reduces the unique bonding that sex can provice in marriage. This undermines the stabilty of marriage when it occurs. *Save sex rather than safe sex should be the ideal being taught....*[S]ex should be considered serious, special or even holy -- in contrast to its trivialization by the media. Instead, the policy [of the Institute of Medicine] accepts casual, non-marital sexual activity as inevitable, thus condoning it with condoms in schools, despite the increases in out-of-wedlock births and sexually transmitted-disease it causes....[T]he highest incidence of sexually transmitted disease occurs among male homosexuals, the leaders of the political movement for sexual freedom with many partners, as opposed to traditional fidelity to one spouse. While better medical information could benefit youngsters, they are much more in need of different school, medical and media *attitudes.*"

Nathaniel S. Lehrman, M.D., Clinical Director, Retired, Kingsboro Psychiatric Center, Brooklyn NY, "Teens and Sex Diseases," *Newsday,* January 13, 1997. (Emphasis ours.)

damage; time alone will not heal the wound. Indeed, a very common factor which we have encountered in the testimonies of homosexuals is the occurrence of unremedied childhood molestation.

Now, More than Ever, Teach Abstinence

On the other hand, a parent *should* avoid overreacting to the discovery that a child has sexually experimented with peers. The bell cannot be "unrung," but a parent can avoid magnifying the bad effects on the child by not reacting too strongly. The best response is to inform all of the parents of the children involved of what has occurred and then to sit down with the child and have a reassuring talk about sexuality and its proper place and time, giving appropriate information to counter any distortions the child has picked up, and listening for emotional reactions to the experience. Included in the discussion should be the message that sex within marriage is a very important, healthy and normal part of a person's life, but that sex outside of marriage can cause terrible problems. (We challenge the reader who may not share this belief to reexamine the issue, keeping their children's emotional health in mind.) Such a talk should be tailored to the age of the child, but should not be delayed out of a belief that a particular child is too young. With the occurrence of a sexual incident, the child *has* become permanently sexually aware.

A parent's job at this stage is to help the child make a commitment to save sex for marriage and to help him understand why this is the very best way to have a happy life. The worst possible outcome is for the child to believe that further sexual experimentation is acceptable. A young child's vista of sexual adventure has even fewer boundaries than an adult's, because his moral standards have not yet been fully formed. The next most harmful result is for the child to believe, because of a parent's inappropriate response, that sex is dirty and secret, so that he learns to associate sexual excitement with shame and to carefully hide his further sexual experimentation.

"At last . . . a book for young people about sex and reproduction in language they can understand, plus pictures they will enjoy." — ANN LANDERS

CHANGING BODIES, GROWING UP, SEX & SEXUAL HEALTH

It's Perfectly Normal

5
Straight and Gay   Page 16
Heterosexuality and Homosexuality

Straight and gay are two words that have to do with sexual desire and sex.
A straight or heterosexual per

A gay or homosexual person is someone who is sexually attracted to people of the same sex. Homos is the ancient Greek

A homosexual relationship between two females is also called a lesbian relationship. The word lesbian began to be used in

ROBI

"Some people disapprove of gay men and lesbian women. Some even hate homosexuals only because they are homosexuals. People may feel this way toward homosexuals because they think homosexuals are different from them or that gay relationships are wrong. Usually these people know little or nothing about homosexuals, and their views are often based on fears or misinformation, not on facts."

Robie H. Harris, *It's Perfectly Normal*, pp. 17-18, 1996.

113

Communicate!

A key to both preventing and to solving problems in our children's lives is good communication. Children are hungry for information and for feedback about their ideas. They seek answers to their many questions. If their parents are accessible and emotionally "safe," that's where they will go to satisfy their communication needs. If the channels of communication are closed or are overly difficult or uncomfortable to access, they will seek answers elsewhere. Good parent/child communication can prevent bad ideas and false information from skewing a child's outlook on life. In the event that faulty thinking somehow "gets past" a mom and dad, good parent/child communication can root it out later when it becomes an issue.

Lots of people in our modern culture have lots of bad ideas they want to teach to our children. The public schools, children's television, and a myriad of media have the ability to bypass parents and take their messages directly to the kids. A parent's best line of defense against harmful information is easy and open communication with his child.

Don't Delay

We have a final and critical word about prevention. We cannot stress too strongly the importance of starting off right with your child at the youngest possible age. The earlier a child begins to be grounded in a healthy sexual identity the better. While almost any unhealthy attitude, habit or belief can be changed with time and effort, it is always sensible to "get it right the first time." There is just no substitute for a good foundation.

Rainbow's End

Free Support/Rap Group

For gay, lesbian, bisexual, and questioning youth, ages 14-21

Every Thursday, 6:30 to 8:30 p.m.

Support

Information   *Exploring Issues*

<u>Facilitators:</u>
Chris Van Stone   For more information
Tom Cantrell   Spectrum   contact Lea Brown
                                                        (415) 457-███.

Communicating about sex to your child;
if you're not doing it, who is?

"Responsible persons are mature people who have taken charge of themselves and their conduct, who *own* their actions and *own up* to them -- who *answer* for them. We help foster a mature sense of responsibility in our children in the same way that we help cultivate other desirable traits: by practice and by example."

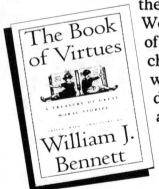

William Bennett, *The Book of Virtues*, p. 186, 1993.

Step Five

IMPROVE YOUR PARENTING SKILLS

In this chapter we turn from a focus on the threats to children which arise from factors outside of the home to the very personal question of how a parent's actions and character can influence a child. Our message might seem old-fashioned or out-of-step with the permissive "baby boomer" generation, yet we believe it will ring true for today's young parents. The dismal results are in on America's permissive attitudes about sex and morality and we believe that young families are looking for something more substantial to build upon. We offer here some tried and true suggestions from earlier times in American culture, yet we offer them with some hesitancy, knowing that post-'60s cultural leaders have worked very long and hard to discredit these ideas. However, if we hope to protect our children from "gay" recruitment we must adopt more family-friendly ways of thinking. We can start by questioning the assumptions about sex and morality which we have been conditioned to accept by the popular culture. Lets face it, after more than 30 years of sexual "revolution," we've all been conditioned to some degree. Nowhere is this more evident than in our reaction to the idea of moral purity.

SELF-DISCIPLINE, COMPASSION, RESPONSIBILITY, FRIENDSHIP, WORK, COURAGE, PERSEVERENCE, HONESTY, LOYALTY, FAITH

Table of Contents from *The Book of Virtues* by William Bennett

"1. TEMPERENCE: Eat not to dullness, drink not to elevation. 2. SILENCE: Speak not but what may benefit others or yourself... 3. ORDER: Let all your things have their places; let each part of your business have its time. 4. RESOLUTION: Resolve to perform what you ought; perform without fail what you resolve. 5. FRUGALITY: ...waste nothing. 6. INDUSTRY: Lose no time... 7. SINCERITY: Use no hurtful deceit... 8. JUSTICE: Wrong none by doing injuries, or omitting the benefits that are your duty. 9. MODERATION: Avoid extremes; forbear resenting injuries as much as you think they deserve. 10. CLEANLINESS: Tolerate no uncleanliness in body, clothes, or habitation. 11. TRANQUILITY: Be not disturbed at trifles, or at accidents common or unavoidable. 12. CHASTITY: Venery [an archaic term for sexual indulgence] but for health or offspring, never to dullness, weakness, or the injury of your own or another's peace or reputation. 13. HUMILITY: Imitate Jesus and Socrates."

Benjamin Franklin, *The Autobiography of Benjamin Franklin*, pp. 80-81, Airmont Publishing, 1965.

The Life of Virtue

Being a good parent is essentially the same as being a good person; a person of virtue. The meaning and the importance of virtue have been somewhat obscured in our morally relativistic society, but basically, virtue is moral excellence and abstinence from vice. Words like virtue and vice, purity, fidelity and chastity seem archaic, even uncomfortable, to modern Americans. Indeed, such terms have fallen almost entirely from common speech except as objects of ridicule, used in the same way that we use the word "goody-goody." What is it about the idea of moral innocence or uprightness that engenders such resentment among "sophisticated" people? Without even having thought about why they do, many people now share this cynicism towards the idea of moral purity. If we did think about it, though. who among us would honestly *not* prefer to marry a virgin, or to have an absolutely, unquestionably faithful spouse as a lifetime partner? Is there anyone who would *not* prefer a business associate of impeccable honesty, or a family doctor, lawyer or accountant whose integrity is beyond question? Putting it another way, would we want to live in a society without people who posses the virtuous qualities that we often mock today? Is it a good sign for our culture (or for our own character) that we do mock them? We need simply point out that as the love of virtue fades, the lure of vice (in all of its forms) grows stronger.

Our Dual Nature

In generations past, Western societies recognized that human beings have a lower nature and a higher nature. The lower nature was associated with selfish appetites and animalistic behavior. The higher nature was associated with altruism and civility. Robert Louis Stevenson's story, *The Strange Case of Dr. Jekyll and Mr. Hyde,* was written to contrast these two inescapable dimensions of human character. The goal of Western civilization has always been to help people to attain greater refinement of character and to overcome their selfish and animalistic tendencies. In America

AMERICAN JEKYLL AND HYDE

"Until the 1950s, as a legacy of the purity movement, America's institutions still largely supported the country's founding ideals of chastity, early childhood modesty, families with a mother and a father, and marital fidelity. After 1950, Dr. Alfred C. Kinsey provided the fraudulent 'scientific' basis required to shift the prevailing standard of judgment regarding human sexuality from a moral standard to a scientifically supported amoral standard of judgment."

Judith Reisman, Ph.D., *R.S.V.P. America*, p. 3, 1996.

"Between these two, I now felt I had to choose. My two natures had memory in common, but all other faculties were most unequally shared between them....To cast in my lot with Jekyll was to die to those appetites which I had long secretly indulged and had of late begun to pamper. To cast it in with Hyde was to die to a thousand interests and aspirations, and to become, at a blow and forever, despised and friendless. The bargain might appear unequal; but there was still another consideration in the scale; for while Jekyll would suffer smartingly in the fires of abstinence, Hyde would not even be conscious of all that he had lost."

Robert Louis Stevenson, *The Strange Case of Dr. Jekyll and Mr. Hyde*, in Charles Neider (ed.), *The Complete Short Stories of Robert Louis Stevenson*, p. 523-4, 1969.

today, however, we seem to have weakened our commitment to uplifting humanity, both corporately and individually, and instead have increasingly embraced coarseness and moral degeneracy. What has been the result? With each passing year the American profile looks a little less like the gentleman, Dr Jekyll, and a little more like the beast, Mr. Hyde.

The decline of civility affects us all. As a parent, however, you have the option of limiting its effects in your home by consciously working to improve your own character and that of your child, instead of "going with the flow" of society.

Pursue Self Improvement

We cannot stress too strongly that we are convinced that a child's best hope for happiness (and his best chance to escape "gay" recruitment) is in living a life of moral uprightness: a life of honesty, integrity and generosity; a life of sexual innocence in youth and sexual faithfulness in marriage. We are aware that these achievements aren't easy; many people have begun to think of them as completely out of reach. A person must first believe that these things are worth having, and then work diligently to achieve them, conquering the powerful temptations and distractions of his own lower nature along the way. The greatest advantage a child can possess in this struggle is to have virtuous parents. On the other hand, the one thing which will rob a child of all enthusiasm for morality is a parent's cynicism. We pointed out earlier that a parent does not need to be morally "spotless" in order to promote the importance of good moral character to his child; he can start by simply believing in that ideal. The next logical step is to work towards making his life conform more closely to the ideal. A child will never fail to be deeply impressed by his parent's sincere efforts to live a better life, though he probably won't talk about it.

Self-improvement is just a process of acknowledging what is true and good and bringing your life into alignment with it. It is a lifelong process, and one which will never meet with complete success. It will bring you into conflict with your lower nature, and

FORMING HABITS

"The experience of pleasure creates powerful, behavior-shaping incentives. For this reason when biological impulses—especially the sexual ones—are not at least partially resisted, trained and brought under the civilizing influence of culture and will, the pressure to seek their immediate fulfillment becomes deeply embedded in the neural network of the brain....What starts out relatively free, becomes less so."

School Sex-Education Guidelines: Teaching About Homosexuality, NARTH publication, 1996.

"You will inevitably adopt the morality of the programs, movies, books, magazines, music, Internet sites and conversations you participate in. GIGO -- Garbage in, garbage out....The cognitive is basic to the behavioral -- you become what you choose to feed your mind on.

Sow A Thought, Reap An Action

Sow An Action, Reap A Habit

Sow A Habit, Reap A Character

Sow A Character, Reap A Destiny"

Randy Alcorn, "Sexual Purity: What You Need to Know," *Eternal Perspectives,* Winter 1997.

sometimes with others around you. But it will also create a roadmap for your child, and it will enable him to respect and trust you. One way to begin is to make a list of virtuous qualities and measure yourself against it every so often, seeing where you have and haven't come closer to your ideal. Benjamin Franklin, that remarkable Founding Father, statesman, newspaperman and inventor, followed such a procedure during his life, and even kept a self-improvement diary.

Embrace Your Parental Role

Along with the self-centeredness of our society has come a view of children as burdens to be endured, rather than treasures to be cherished. American society has given birth to a major industry, day care, whose sole purpose is to warehouse children for working parents. In today's economic climate many parents feel that they have no other choice but to earn two incomes, placing their kids in day care. What factors created this problem? Starting in the '60s, many women left the home and their primary role as full-time moms to enter the work force, believing that they would reap personal fulfillment as well as the additional income to improve the economic status of their families. Market forces soon drove up housing and other family costs in response to the buying power of two-parent working families. Taxation at all levels also rose steadily. Now families virtually *require* two wage earners to provide what once could be provided by only one. Those who choose to keep one parent at home to raise their children must often sacrifice financially to do so.

Parents caught in this double bind tend to bring their attitudes in line with their necessity: they justify working by reasoning that they can "give" their children more. We now have a society in which couples are willing to trade their children's daily home-life for what they perceive as a higher standard of living. Such a trade-off reveals a great blindness among American parents to the richness and fulfillment which accrues to each member of a truly family-centered home.

WHAT SUCCESS REALLY IS

"Increasingly, our sick culture has dismissed the importance of family and home in favor of a seductive upward mobility. Children are to be shunted aside in favor of that old goddess Success, and if you seek the results, just look around. Any parent who has ever left a little one off at day care for the first time and has seen the look in the kid's eyes knows what I'm talking about. But it is now mindlessly assumed that no success in the home is worth losing out on the rewards offered by the glittering world outside, when in reality no success in business or politics or professional career can make up for failure in the home. Ask anybody who's had a child go astray or lost children through divorce or who can't find peace or even time at home. No amount of fragile success can make up for such a loss. Or its repercussions....It's not just children who learn from parents, but parents from children. They renew us callow adults, keep wonder and curiosity alive and remind us of what is truly important, and what success really is."

Paul Greenberg, *Arkansas Democrat-Gazette*, reprinted in *American Family Association Journal*, May, 1998.

Family Time -- Burden or Blessing?

A corollary of this attitude is the notion that family time is not nearly so fulfilling as "personal time" and individual pursuits. Helped along by constant media messages (consider images of family life in "The Simpsons"), this belief holds that families are just a collection of individuals who occupy the same space, and who would all prefer to be off doing their own thing. In fact, they would be much better off doing so, if we believe the depictions of intra-family disrespect, inconsiderateness and conflict in the sitcoms. We have known even stay-at-home moms who spend most of every day ferrying children to school, sports, lessons, clubs, parties and entertainment events -- an endless string of non-family activities which eat up every moment of potential family time -- and feel that the high point of the day is getting a moment for their own personal pursuits, or simply time alone.

What we criticize here is not people's individual hobbies and interests, but the *attitude* that devalues the fun and irreplaceable experiences of family life in favor of exclusively individual interests. Remember that this book seeks to offer solutions to a psychosexual disorder that is often rooted in missing or inadequate family connections. How can any family member make those deep and necessary connections, indeed even enjoy life fully, if he is left out or pushed out of his family to find fulfillment?

Once again, fathers are often the big losers in this scenario. When a father defines himself primarily as breadwinner and spouse, or as fill-in-support-parent for his working wife, he has defined himself out of the most important role in his life. How often do we hear the term "baby-sitting" used to describe the periods of time when fathers watch their children? A father isn't "baby-sitting" at such times, he is parenting!

Moms and dads should reject both the "me-first" and the "every-man-for-himself" mind-sets of our society and embrace their family relationships with pleasure and enthusiasm. In a healthy family the time spent with a spouse and children offers much more in the way of happiness and personal satisfaction than any consumer

QUESTION AUTHORITY

"On behalf of the Council on Families, I recently conducted a study of 20 of the most current and widely-available college textbooks on marriage and family life. As someone who has taught these courses for 20 years, I was aware that such textbooks have shortcomings. But what I found was worse than I had expected. Taken as a whole, these books are a national embarrassment. They are full of glaring errors, distortions of research, omissions of important data, and misattributions of scholarship. Most of all, they are shot through with the idea that marriage is not a particularly worthwhile institution.

An anthropologist from Mars who read these textbooks would come away with several basic beliefs. First, in America, marriage is just one of many equally acceptable and productive ways of finding a partner and raising children. In fact, if anything, marriage as a lifelong bond based on child-rearing holds special dangers for women, who are likely to find marriage physically threatening, psychologically stifling, or both. Those Americans who suspect otherwise, according to these books, have had their brains befuddled by various 'myths,' which modern science has definitely refuted.

Moreover, the story continues, there is little evidence that divorce or unwed motherhood harms children or society. Instead, the more pressing danger comes from negative stereotypes about alternate family forms, which may encourage racial prejudice and reinforce social pressure that prevents us as individuals from freely choosing....It is highly revealing that almost all 20 books take this view on virtually every question...What is presented in these books as an 'expert consensus' is sharply at odds with much of the weight of social science evidence...Do textbooks matter? You bet they do. And until publishers, instructors, and textbook authors clean up their act, the best advice I can give...is: Question authority. Almost certainly, you have been exposed to misinformation -- and worse -- on many important topics."

Sociologist Noval Glenn, University of Texas, Los Angeles Times, 9-16-97.

product does. What is more, a parent's investment in a child offers a continuing, valuable return, as a child grows over the years from a baby to a playmate to a protégé to a friend and hopefully, along the way, to a fellow parent, widening the circle of joy yet further by bringing grandchildren into the family. How quick we are to accept the splitting apart of the natural family into merely individual and self-centered components. How quick we are to accept fool's gold when we have genuine treasure in our families.

Effective Parental Attitudes

We continue this chapter with some words of wisdom from Alan Medinger, a leader in the homosexual recovery movement. The following is taken from an article called "How to Raise a Heterosexual Child" from *Regeneration News*. Alan's group, Regeneration, is a Christian ministry organization and thus his article has a Christian emphasis, but the principles which it identifies apply to families of all faiths.

"If only..." – two of the saddest words in the English language....Often, they come from a parent who sees how he could have treated that one child a little differently, and perhaps homosexuality might never have been an issue. We can't go back and live our lives over again, and if we are parents of grown children, it is not likely we will be parents again, so with the Lord's help we deal as best we can with the reality that is. But, in a ministry like Regeneration, we can do some prevention work. That opportunity comes when we get to address new parents or parents-to-be. This article is intended to be preventative; it is addressed to parents [and others] who have an influence on the development of a young child....I believe [that the following parenting guidelines] will foster a child's growing up with a healthy sexual identity....

PASSING A BROKEN BATON

"The true feminine, I think has been lost. Today's feminist is angry, aggressive, masculinized, and has lost her sacred place in the home....Mothers who cannot honor the feminine in their own natures become unavailable, dull, depressed, angry, compulsive -- living by neurotic rituals which they use in order to fill the empty core of their being. Their daughters are wounded by this. And so the daughters carry on this wound to the feminine spirit for yet another generation."

Psychotherapist Diane Eller-Boyko, Interview, *NARTH Bulletin*, April 1998.

"Generally, the findings [of several major studies] tend to be in agreement with Freud's idea of a 'negative father.' It is noteworthy that the same result emerged for males. Both female and male homosexuals apparently felt highly estranged from their fathers."

Seymour Fisher and Roger Greenberg, *Freud Scientifically Reappraised: Testing the Theories and Therapy*, 1996.

"Research shows that boys with involved fathers do better in school, have higher self-esteem and less anti-social behavior. Girls with involved fathers tend not to be premature parents. They're not looking in the wrong places for that missing male love."

Jane Fonda, Speech to the Georgia Campaign for Adolescent Pregnancy Prevention, *Leadership Bulletin*, 11-12, 1997. In AFA Journal, May 1998.

1. Both mother and father have clearly defined roles.

A child, to a significant degree, takes his or her sexual identity through bonding with the same sex parent....Imagine the confusion that arises when the parents' roles are uncertain or indistinct, or worse, the object of control battles.

2. The father affirms his son in his maleness, and his daughter in her femininity.

We have all seen how the little boy bends his arm to show his dad his muscle. Implied is the plea, "Tell me I'm a man." Confidence in our manhood is a fragile thing in most men, gay or straight, but in the little boy in his formative years, the need to be affirmed in his manhood by the one who is his symbol of manhood, is vital. We have also seen how important the role of the father is in affirming the role of the daughter in her femininity. When she is his "little princess," when those things that make her distinctly feminine are valued by her father, then she herself starts to value being a woman. Affirmation is expressed in daily life when the parents show the expectation that the son or daughter will one day fulfill the defined male and female roles modeled by their parents. Thus, the father apprentices his son and the mother her daughter in "the things that we men (women) do".

3. The father is involved in the life of the family and exercises [leadership].

The book, Deadly Secrets, is a tragic account of a Christian man who died of AIDS after living in a secret homosexual life. What makes the book extraordinary is that it is based on journals the man started keeping in his early teens. Although he probably did not recognize the significance of his observation at the time, in several instances of family crisis, he described how his dad was "reading the paper". We encounter far more workaholic than alcoholic

THE COMMUNICATION BREAKDOWN

"When it comes to self, the world around them, and the future, a new study found the views of teenagers and adults nearly mirror each other in their positive outlook. But whan it comes to how teens believe adults feel towards them, the picture abruptly darkens. According to a survey by the Barna Research Group of Oxnard, California, most teens have a healthy and positive self-image ....However, when teens were asked to choose words that described how they thought most adults felt about them, a disturbing negative picture appeared. Most believed adults viewed teenagers as 'lazy' (84%), 'rude' (74%), 'dishonest' (65%), and 'violent' (57%)....A news release by Barna Research said the survey showed that teenagers 'have a sense of unease about adults....Without a sense of acceptance and respect, young people are not prone to submitting themselves to the leadership of people or organizations that have failed to embrace them.' George Barna, president of the research group, added, 'our most recent surveys among teens also underscore their overwhelming desire to be unconditionally accepted by their family, particularly by their parents.'"

AFA Journal, May 1998

fathers among the men and women to whom we minister. Among men we encounter far more with a physically abusive father. "Dad was there, but not there," is the description of early life we hear over and over again. Involvement by the father in the life of the child is in itself a form of affirmation, and conveys worth to the child, not just as a person, but as a man or woman.

4. The father loves the mother.

For the young girl, it is obvious how important this is. In showing love for his wife, the father creates the climate in which the little girl can believe it is safe and good to be a woman. Men can be trusted. For the boy, the father who loves the mother models what it is for a man to go beyond himself. The boy sees an example of a man free from the narcissism that is so common to male youths and characterizes the immaturity of so many grown men today. A man who loves his wife, and cherishes her and protects her, embodies masculine strength. The boy will want to model this.

5. The mother shows esteem for the father.

For the daughter, the mother's respect again shows that men are to be trusted; that it is good and safe to be a woman. The mother's view of the father can become her view of him – and her view of men in general. The boy is receiving messages from both parents, and his mother's view of the father will help shape his view of manhood. Perhaps even more important, a father who is belittled by the mother, whether he accepts it or fights back, provides a poor model for a young boy. A weak father who accepts contempt, or a father who fights back, can both lead the boy to choose to identify with the mother, more than with the father.

TESTIMONIAL

"My father worked for the Y.M.C.A. as head of the Boys Department. As his son, I enjoyed a sense of 'privilege' being the 'boss" son. There was ping-pong and pool tables, board games, T.V., occasional movies....I loved exploring the old "Y" building, with its hotel, dining rooms, meeting halls and large staircases. Eventually I explored without anyone noticing me, often spending time up on the roof. This time of marvelous wonder was ruined for me. One day I was molested by a man in an out-of-the-way rest-room....Curiosity led me into the encounter; the physical sensations were subtle and enticing enough to keep me interested. But more importantly, an adult was spending time with me, being intimate with me, touching me! Obviously, my need for this sort of 'male bonding' was great. I always felt I was a disappointment to my father, being sick, prone to crying and being 'effeminate.' His need as a man and father seemed adequately met by working with the other boys; we never spent much 'quality time' doing stuff together. If we did, I usually tried his patience to the limit."

D.L. "Sonny" Weaver, "Through the Valley of Death, to Hell and Back!: One Christian Man's Struggle with Alcohol, Drugs and Homosexuality." pages 1-2, 1990.

6. The parents respect the dignity and individuality of each child.

Although important in all parent-child relationships, this seems especially critical with mothers and sons. The process of growth into manhood for a boy is a series of creating and breaking bonds. Coming from the mother's body, the boy at first identifies with the mother. At some point he must break free from her and bond with the father, and eventually he breaks free from the father and becomes his own man. Sometimes the neediness of the mother does not allow the independence of the son to develop. Unhealthy bonds keep him tied to her, often as a best friend or substitute [for her] husband...

7. Both parents acknowledge [traditional] moral values.

...To apply moral values in the home is to provide a safe channel in which a child can grow, with the understanding that outside the channel lies danger. In a world that declares there are no absolutes and proclaims that real freedom is experienced by escaping from the restrictions of the past, the danger to our children is enormous. [Modern society tells] our children that homosexuality is a perfectly legitimate option, and so, without moral teaching in the home, it becomes simply one of the options they can choose, one that at some stages of development and in some situations might seem quite attractive....

Seven Steps to Recruit-Proof Your Child

414 MASON STREET, SAN FRANCISCO, CA 94102

BIG BROTHERS/ BIG SISTERS
OF SAN FRANCISCO

August 9, 1991

Mr. Charles A. Lynch
Chairman of the Board
United Way of the Bay Area
410 Bush Street
San Francisco, CA 94108

Dear Mr. Lynch:

The Board of Directors of Big Brothers / Big Sisters of San Francisco wish to convey our support to you and The United Way concerning the special task force recently commissioned to determine The United Way's long-term relationship with the Boy Scouts of America. This matter has been discussed at our recent Committee meeting and has received unqualified support.

We are confident that solutions exist to resolve the current impasse between the Boy Scouts and the gay community. Our confidence is based on more than 11 years experience with gay, bisexual and lesbian Big Brother and Big Sister volunteers. We know, for example, that a nondiscrimination practice in the use of "non-traditional" volunteers in the service delivery to youth can serve the best interest of children. Indeed, this should be the only criterion for methods and practices concerning service to youth. A nondiscriminatory policy need not be viewed as a political concession to focussed community pressures.

ADVICE TO SINGLE PARENTS

A single parent faces special challenges in the struggle to protect a child from "gay" recruitment. Although some parents prefer not to believe it, a child invariably suffers emotional harm from the breakup of his family, whether from death, divorce or abandonment. This emotional trauma may make a child more vulnerable to recruitment. In addition, a single parent has less time, energy and resources than a married couple does and may therefore be less able to keep as close a watch over the child as is prudent. Every factor which threatens a child in an intact home is compounded in a broken home. On top of this, sexual predators are well aware of these facts and use them to their advantage. But don't lose hope! You *can* recruit-proof your child; it's just going to take some extra effort. There are a few basic rules.

Don't Dis the Ex

This is a commonly-expressed rule for divorced parents, but one they usually find tough to follow. You must separate your feelings about your broken marriage relationship from your child's relationship with his mom or dad. Many divorced parents define their child's needs in ways that that justify their own hostile feelings and actions towards their estranged spouse. Understandably, they may have a hard time being objective, but that's no excuse for hurting their child. In the worst-case scenario, a parent will deliberately use a child to hurt the other parent. More commonly, the parent, transferring his own anger and pain onto the child, simply decides that the child is "better off" without having the other parent around. Try to help your child get the most out of his relationship with his other parent. If possible, work together with your ex-spouse to establish consistent rules and a coordinated parenting strategy to care for the child. Take some time, if necessary, to come to terms with the fact that you will be linked to your former spouse through your child for a lifetime. Sometimes, simply accepting this fact makes it easier to have the wisdom to do what's best.

INFILTRATION OF YOUTH ORGANIZATIONS

"The Girl Scouts allows lesbian leaders in its organization and has expelled at least one heterosexual leader who refused to keep this policy secret from parents. Brenda Mailand, a Girl Scout employee in Lansing, Michigan, was fired after she refused to sign the following pledge:

'As an employee of the Michigan Capitol Girl Scout Council, you may not proactively inform members, parents of members or prospective members, or members of the general public (including media) of the Council's and GSUSA's position on sexual orientation.'"

Private Letter, February 9, 1993, In Scott Lively and Kevin Abrams, *The Pink Swastika*, p.198-199, 1997.

"Big Brothers/Big Sisters of America...welcomes gay and lesbian participants....Beth Anderson, program director of Big Brothers of King County in Seattle explained, 'We felt that we were closing the door on a lot of potential volunteers.' Anderson stressed that the decision to accept a gay man as a Big Brother is left up to the child's parent, but added, 'If we felt that someone was being really close-minded or had misconceptions (about gay people), we might try to educate them a bit.'"

Just Out, March 1, 1993.

Fill the Empty Shoes

In situations in which the child's same-sex parent is unavailable, find a replacement to substitute in the parental gender role (to do boy or girl things together). Many single parents get closer to their sibling's families so that the child can spend quality "gender-affirming" time with an uncle or aunt. Often a grandparent will fill in as a role model (in such a situation you may need to ask him or her to be more "parental" and less indulgent than a grandparent might otherwise be). Church families can be very valuable resources for single-parent families in many ways (if they are genuinely family centered -- watch out for pro-"gay" congregations). When forming connections with strangers (or even with friends and family members you don't know very well) on behalf of your child, be aware that sexual predators and others may take advantage of your situation to get close to your child for their own reasons. Be especially careful of youth-oriented organizations such as Big Brothers/Big Sisters, and Girl Scouts. The "gay" movement has infiltrated many of these organizations, which now allow homosexual leaders (although parents are often not informed of this). Boy Scouts has been very vigilant on this score.

From the newsletter of the Human Rights Campaign, Fall 1995

"Shaping the lives of children is the most important job in society. It must be approached with diligence. Phil Esposito, the famous hockey player, gave an example of this dedication when he was asked where he learned to play. 'At home in the basement,' he responded. 'My mother was the goalie. She was the typical Italian mother, nothing got past her!'"

Nicholas Puiia, *Rules For The Traditional Family*, p. 31, 1988.

Step Six

CLEAN HOUSE

Positive Change Takes Effort

An essential part of any effort to recruit-proof a child is to limit his exposure to pro-"gay" influences. Such influences are so pervasive in our culture today that it would be nearly impossible to remove them all from a child's environment, so we will limit our discussion to the most harmful of them. Unfortunately, the most harmful pro-homosexual influences may be the ones that a parent finds the most difficult to remove (even if he already desires to do so). Hopefully, the knowledge that some changes will help a child avoid "gay" recruitment will make them easier for parents to carry out.

Be Protective

A common myth of parenting is that parents shouldn't be protective of their children, but should allow them to experience life on its own terms. This attitude might have been acceptable in earlier years in a rural America where even total strangers could usually be counted on to look out for a child's welfare, but it is not acceptable today. The parent who, in this day and age, chooses to let a child experience life on its own terms courts disaster. If ever there were a

ONE FAMILY'S EXPERIENCE WITH A GAY TEACHER
From testimony to Congress, C-Span, April 2, 1998.

"On April 30, 1997, after the coming out episode of *Ellen*, a fifth grade teacher of my daughter [Heather]...proceeded to lead a class 'discussion' on *Ellen*, in direct violation of our signed form [opting our children out of any classroom presentations of homosexual material]. She wrote the words 'brave' and 'proud' on the board, and placed a big star by the word 'brave.' She went on to say that she was very proud of Ellen for saying she was gay....The teacher wrote on the board that out of every 100 kids, 63% are gay. At that comment, my daughter shook her head no in disagreement....The teacher ended the "discussion" by asking the children in the class, who agreed with her that Ellen was brave for saying she was gay. My daughter was one of three children who did not raise their hands. The teacher then asked my daughter directly what she thought. My daughter told her she disagreed. When the teacher began to pressure her for an answer, my daugher broke down into tears, feeling humiliated." Mike Trelow, parent, Alameda, California.

"When I found out I was in this teacher's class I was very excited, because she was fun and had a lot of great things to do....I had heard rumors about her being a lesbian but I didn't want to believe this about her....On [that day in class] I was crushed to see and hear what she was writing on the board and talking about....I knew she was teaching against my beliefs and what my parents had taught me, and she knew it was against my beliefs. I now feel ashamed of her and hurt that she could even bring that into our class and discuss it....She should not be a teacher because she wanted me to obey her in thinking that gay was O.K." Heather Trelow, fifth grade.

time for parents to be protective of their children, this is it.

"Protective" doesn't describe a parent who tries to shelter a child from all experience; it describes one who guides the child through experiences with a loving hand. A protective parent shields his child from unhealthy influences and actively intervenes on the child's behalf in every instance in which the child will encounter a potentially dangerous and hostile environment. Where there is no genuine danger, he stands back and lets the child learn his own lessons, but where there *is* danger, he walks with the child, pointing out the right path and the hazards to avoid.

Know Your Adversary

In ancient Athens, there were many adults who sought children and adolescents for their sexual gratification. Pederasty became such a threat to children that all parents who could afford to hired chaperones to escort their children to school and back. Their culture was like ours in the sense that sexual freedom had gotten so out of hand that children were continually threatened by the number and the boldness of sexual predators in their communities. Today in America, people whose plans include the sexualization of children are quite possibly more prevalent than they were in ancient Greece, but they aren't necessarily lurking in the bushes waiting for children to walk home from school. Today they occupy positions of influence throughout the society. They are educators, activists in news and entertainment media, leaders in youth organizations, and government and academic sexuality "experts" who design and implement every type of sex-related program in which children are involved. In fact, there is no field relating to children which does not have its share of these determined and often influential people, working hard throughout their lifetimes to gain a society free from any form of sexual "repression." A parent should not blindly allow his child to learn the lessons which these people fervently wish to teach him.

FROM TOLERANCE TO TOTALITARIANISM

"[We must present] positive images of homosexuality in school curricula....Anti-bias curricula must be introduced as early as kindergarten and must continue through high school."

Karen Franklin, Washington University, from a Congressional briefing on "hate crimes." In *Traditional Values Report*, Winter 1998.

"If parents are allowed to have their children opt out of gay and lesbian units, what will happen when we teach about Dutch culture or African-American history? It scares me."

First-grade teacher, Hawthorne Elementary School, Madison, Wisconsin, from *It's Elementary: Talking About Gay Issues in School,* a training video for pro-"gay" educators.

"Not only in California, but across the nation, state and municipal laws encourage parents to exercise the extraordinary option of REMOVING children from discussions of homosexuality...Encourage your local officials to oppose such 'opt-out' policies...which ultimately deny EVERY student's right to an education free of unchallenged bigotry."

Gay and Lesbian Alliance Against Defamation (GLADD) statement, P.E.R.S.O.N. Project Home Page, www.youth.org. 1997.

Take Your Child Out of Public School (if you can).

One of the most harmful threats to a child's sexual health is the public school environment. Modern public schools have become an emotional jungle for children in which both peer pressure and the teaching of unconventional sexual values conspire to quickly rob a child of sexual innocence. The typical peer group alone is capable of undoing much of the moral training that a child receives in the home. This process is accelerated by public school policies based on the belief that sexual behavior by young people is not only acceptable but inevitable. The nature of our popular culture is such that some parents have not been overly concerned about educators' permissive attitudes towards heterosexual behavior. Now the circle of tolerance has been widened to embrace homosexual behavior as well. Many public schools have become active centers of "gay" propaganda, in which children are taught to view homosexual behavior as healthy and normal and are sometimes humiliated for expressing intolerance of homosexuality. Sadly, the climate is not much different in many private schools (excepting those with strong religious emphasis or very high levels of parental involvement). The problem seems to arise as much from the nature of group education in a culture with declining values as it does from the dysfunctional state of public education.

The Homeschool Advantage

In response to the deteriorating academic and moral standards which exist in public schools today, many parents have opted to teach their children at home. More than one million families currently home-school in the United States. Parents have learned that easy-to-get prepackaged curriculum materials can help anyone teach his own children effectively. Researchers have discovered that not only do children learn better (scoring higher on standardized tests) under the tutelage of the people who love them the most, but both the level and kind of social skills they acquire are markedly superior to those of their public school counterparts.

"GAY" CHIC
THE NEW WAY TO GET ATTENTION
(OR TO GET BACK AT YOUR PARENTS)

"In 1993, *Gentlemen's Quarterly* published a cover story on 'The Straight Queer' -- detailing how 'many prominent heterosexuals are aping the gay sensibility as a kind of grand fashion.' A figure from New York's drag scene became a fixture in *The New York Times* "Style" section. *New York* magazine ran a cover story called 'Lesbian Chic.' A straight rock musician named Kurt Cobain admitted he was 'definitely gay in spirit' some months before he took his own life. Barbra Streisand and Elizabeth Taylor became active in gay causes. A good many college students were pretending to be gay. In November 1993, *Newsweek* reported that 'at high schools around the country, multiculturism has begun to embrace multisexualism. With or without official blessing, student gay organizations have cropped up in Chicago, Berkeley, Miami, Minneapolis, New York. In Massachusetts alone, more than a hundred public and private schools have such groups, including George Bush's alma mater, Andover.'"

Charles W. Socarides, M.D., *Homosexuality -- A Freedom Too Far, p. 12, 1995.*

Home-schooled children tend to be more self-assured and less easily swayed by harmful peer pressure. Additionally, they interact better with adults, and do not develop the distrust and disrespect for authority that has become so common among public school children. Combined with group sports, scouting and other extracurricular activities, homeschooling gives a child everything he needs in the way of educational and social development without causing him to lose his positive self-image, his independent judgment, or his moral bearings along the way.

Rebellious Kids Are Made, Not Born

One of the most startling discoveries of the home-school movement is that (contrary to the conventional "wisdom") children do not have to be rebellious or at odds with their families at any age, even in their teen years. For the most part, teenagers who have been home-schooled from early childhood are surprisingly cooperative and pleasant human beings, perhaps because they perceive their parents as their advocates rather than their adversaries. The idea of having peaceful, close-knit families during their children's teenage years should be especially appealing to parents today. Incidentally, teenage rebelliousness among public school children has increasingly begun to manifest itself as "in-your-face" homosexual behavior, especially among girls.

Although a number of parents don't have the option of withdrawing their children from public school, we believe that most parents actually do have alternatives. A simple rearrangement of priorities and a willingness to rethink their material ambitions would allow many parents to protect their children from the effects of public education, both social and academic. In cases in which one parent can stay home (and most families — with careful budgeting — find that their standard of living stays about the same even without the second income), homeschooling is an excellent option. Homeschooling also works for many parents who work out of their home or who work part-time. Another option is private schooling, especially if your locality offers a voucher option, but we caution

EXTENDING THE SEXUAL REVOLUTION

"[Sex education programs of the future] will probe sexual expression...across...generational lines."

Lester Kirkendall, *Journal of Sex Education and Therapy*, Spring/Summer 1985.

"The unifying core of...sex education is not intellectual but ideological. Its mission is to defend and extend ...the sexual revolution."

Barbara DaFoe Whitehead, *Atlantic Monthly*, October 1994.

"Without advance notice, which might have given parents some hint of what was coming, all students were ordered to attend a 90 minute presentation by Hot, Sexy and Safer Productions, Inc...[Owner Suzi] Landolphi told the students they were going to have a 'group sexual experience'; she advocated and approved oral sex, masturbation, homosexual sexual activity, and condom use during promiscuous premarital sex; she simulated masturbation...She referred to being in 'deep sh—' after anal sex; she had a male minor lick an oversize condom with her, after which she had a female minor pull it over the male minor's entire head; she encouraged a male minor to display his 'orgasm face' with her for the camera, and she informed him he was not having enough orgasms."

Human Events, December 29, 1995.

you to be extremely selective! Some private schools operate on an even more radical version of the social engineering philosophy we have encountered in the public schools.

Active Parenting Is the Next-Best Thing

For those who *are* limited to the public school option, active parental involvement is essential. Active parenting requires more than simply attending parent-teacher conferences, it requires an exercise of parental authority over the school environment itself. If you limit your interaction with the school system to the forums offered by school officials, you may come away with a false sense of security; controlled forums allow activist teachers to hide things which might offend parents. Many educators and school administrators believe and act on the assumption that a child becomes their property once he has passed through the schoolhouse door. Such an attitude, combined with strongly "politically correct" values, causes some of these educators to view the moral reeducation of children as their fundamental duty. Parents in our present-day moral culture should not be passive consumers, content to accept every official communication and decision at face value; they should become informed and powerful advocates for their children.

No Public School Sex Education

Everything a child needs to know about the mechanics of sexuality can be imparted in a half-hour conversation with his parent. The physical aspect of human sexuality is not at all complicated. If a school finds it necessary to schedule hours of class time to provide sex education for your child, then he is probably being taught specific behaviors and values. Do you really want to trust a stranger to teach your child someone else's version of sexual values and behavior? Especially the version of someone with a social agenda? America's leading sex educators do indeed have an agenda, and virtually all of them embrace Kinseyan sexual theory.

GAY SEX-ED IN NON-SEX-ED CLASSES

"Aside from *The Catcher in the Rye* (which alludes peripherally to homosexuality), Larry Kramer's play, *The Normal Heart* was the first work I taught that centered on gay life...I was also pushing myself to...cross the boundaries that seemed to be set in unspoken stone. If anyone did want to voice objections, I readied myself with answers framed in language designed to set people at ease...In a senior elective course called "Images of Women," I set Rita Mae Brown's *Rubyfruit Jungle* and Gloria Naylor's *The Women of Brewster Place* alongside the stories of D.H. Lawrence, Ernest Hemingway and Charlotte Bronte's *Jane Eyre*. *The emphasis these texts placed on sexual awakening as a rite of passage and independence as the result of coming of age makes them rich with relevance for high school seniors.*"

Homosexualist Nancy Boutilier, "Reading, Writing and Rubyfruit Jungle: High School Students Respond to Gay and Lesbian Literature," *Out/Look*, Winter 1992 (Emphasis ours).

"Four gay ghosts with purple faces met six gay ghosts with bright green faces. They all hid in a great big pumpkin. How many ghosts were hiding in the pumpkin? _____"

First grade math worksheet, Clackamas County, Oregon, 1992. ("Teacher, what does 'gay' mean?").

(We should mention that a frightening number of these "experts" *openly* advocate adult-child sex). These men and women design and write most of the sex education curricula used in American public schools.

A parent's best strategy in dealing with sex education is to alert school officials in advance that his child is not to be instructed about sexuality in school, either during regular classes or during special events or outings. We recommend that you do not wait until the issue arises during the school year. Activist teachers are specially trained by their special interest groups to circumvent parents. For example, regarding pro-"gay" instruction to children, the lesbian founder of Project 10 (an aggressive "gay" recruitment program for public schools), advises teachers to push through their agenda first and apologize later for not asking for permission. Unfortunately, "sorry" doesn't undo the damage to kids' emotions and attitudes.

Providing unequivocal instructions (preferably in writing) to school officials before any incident occurs is the only sure method of thwarting the possible sex education plans of activists. (Such an approach may also preserve a parent's legal standing in the event that his instructions are ignored).

Shut Off the TV

Almost as harmful to young people's sexual health is today's television programming, where rank lewdness passes for humor in every situation comedy and "artistic" depictions of depravity pass for sophistication on "highbrow" public broadcasting stations. Increasingly, television shows are laced with pro-"gay" propaganda, and familiar T.V. faces are identified as active homosexuals. "Ellen" was the most blatant of the self-identified homosexuals on television. The "Ellen" show's "coming out" episode, with its enormous vanguard of media hype, demonstrated the power of the "gay" movement to force its agenda into prime-time programming. And, though the show's viewership later dwindled, the public's interest in that episode showed the ability of "gay" activists to gain the willing attention of the prime-time audience. The demise of

The Gay Mafia

Capo di tutti

Who are the real power brokers in Hollywood and how much do they *really* control? MARK EBNER peeks over the lavender walls of Tinseltown.

Spy May/June 1995

"The average American household watches over seven hours of TV daily. Those hours open up a gateway into the private world of straights, through which a Trojan horse might be passed. As far as desensitization is concerned, the medium *is* the message -- of normalcy. So far, gay Hollywood has provided our best covert weapon in the battle to desensitize the mainstream."

Marshall Kirk and Erastus Pill, "The Overhauling of Straight America," *Guide Magazine*, November 1987.

"Ellen" was not in any sense a serious setback for the "gay" movement. Whereas the show proved to be too heavy a dose of "gay" propaganda for most viewers, it lasted long enough to achieve its intended effect: to desensitize the public about homosexuality on television, and to make other pro-"gay" efforts seem more palatable by comparison.

The "Opiate of the Masses"

The important fact to keep in mind about television viewing is that it puts children under the near-hypnotic influence of this nation's most dedicated and persuasive homosexualists. Karl Marx described religion as the opiate of the masses, but no religion has ever come close to having the powerful narcotic effect of television. And who controls this medium of indoctrination? Unarguably, the people with the greatest control over television are the same sort of "politically correct" social activists who embrace the cause of "gay rights" as their own. The larger part of their programming appears to cater to middle-class values, but many shows have become vehicles for social change, especially change in favor of the "gay" political agenda.

Parents should keep in mind the power of repetition in selling an idea. We are very familiar with this phenomenon in Hitler's "big lie" tactic (repeat a lie often enough and most people will believe it) and in consumer advertising (we've all memorized dozens of useless jingles just by hearing them over and over). However, the process of repetition can be used to sell *any* message. Although we probably all recognize the process in television advertising, we may be less conscious of the use of repetition in television shows themselves to "sell" us *attitudes* about morals, values and behaviors. Social activists, such as homosexualist scriptwriters and program directors, use their positions to ensure that television "heroes" uniformly exhibit "politically correct" attitudes and views, while "villains" always profess "politically *in*correct" attitudes and views. The continual repetition of these themes helps to shape the attitudes of television viewers themselves, often without them noticing it.

WEANED FROM THE "BOOB TUBE"

We offer this from nationally known family psychologist and columnist Dr. John Rosemond: " After eight years of no television, Jim Wilson of Allen, Texas wrote:

'Before we eliminated television, we had noticed the kinds of problems you mentioned in your article: short attention spans, irritability, lack of cooperation, and chronic boredom. Today, nearly every one of our five children - who range in ages from 6 to 17 - are straight-A students. Off TV, they quickly developed a variety of interests, including sports, reading, art, computing, etc. I listen to my neighbors and associates bemoan their family problems, including their childrens' difficulties with attention deficit disorder, discipline and underachievement in school. In their home, the television is on almost constantly and everyone's addicted to it, but my friends don't seem to get the connection. I'm sure glad we did.'

'Dr. Rosemond writes that once 'withdrawal' has run its course (this usually takes 4-6 weeks), parents report significant, often times dramatic improvements in behavior, sibling relationships, and attitudes toward school. He concludes: 'Not at all uncommon are stories of children with attention deficit-hyperactivity disorder whose symptoms improve remarkably and sometimes all but disappear within a relatively short period of time.'"

Reprinted from *American Family Association Journal*, August 1996

Due to the pervasiveness of "political correctness" in television programming, "selective" viewing may not be an entirely effective means of avoiding pro-"gay" indoctrination. There is also the problem that offensive programs are often advertised during more acceptable programs. These "promos" often contain some of the most offensive material and appear without warning during commercial breaks. Consumer product advertising also frequently contains offensive messages and imagery. One solution for families is to limit their television viewing to movie rentals; these have no commercial interruptions and parents can fast-forward past inappropriate scenes. In like manner, parents can fast-forward through objectionable parts of television programs if they tape them for later viewing.

The TV-Free Home

Not surprisingly, children who learn to get along without television tend to be better thinkers, readers, conversationalists and self-motivators. And shifting to a less TV-dominated lifestyle is not as difficult for children as you might think. Initial television withdrawal pains are quickly replaced by a newfound appreciation for books, hobbies and active play. Even teenagers can be weaned off the "boob tube" but as with most of the suggestions in this book, the younger the child, the more certain the positive effect. In our own home, the bookshelf gets more use than the television, although we enjoy lots of good movies from the video store.

No Pornography

Pornography is not only detrimental to the men who use it and the women who are exploited in its production, but the very presence of pornography in a home where there are children can contribute to their vulnerability to "gay" recruitment. We have pointed out that "gay" recruitment is fundamentally a process of changing a person's attitude about sexuality. As with TV, any influence which promotes the concept of sexual freedom outside of

Leading Homosexual Groups Sponsor Event Exposing Students to Hard-Core Porn

X-Rated, Sadomasochistic Flicks, Session Led by Prostitute

by Peter LaBarbera
LAMBDA REPORT EXCLUSIVE

SANTA CRUZ, CA — Two leading homosexual activist groups sponsored a conference at the University of California at Santa Cruz that exposed college and high school students to hard-core pornography, sadomasochistic films, and a workshop on "Sex Workers" led by a prostitute.

The conference was sponsored by the Human Rights Campaign, the nation's most high-profile homosexual group videos. An *LR* reporter attended

"Pornographers [have replaced] the notion of 'creational sex' with Kinsey's 'recreational sex' Recreational sex became a hit with single college men and any hesitancy they felt was usually dispelled by their social science professors, who by then were parroting Kinsey's variant view of sexuality. Both the sexual philosophy purveyed by Kinsey and the pornographic value system are heterophobic. Both teach distrust and fear toward the opposite sex. Walter Allen said in 1962; 'Pornography is transcribed masturbation fantasy.' It turns out that while this sexual variant may not cause warts or insanity, it does encourage a selfish sexual autonomy, the breaking down of moral barriers and taboos and the building up of other barriers and taboos."

Judith Reismen, PhD, *R.S.V.P. America,* p. 28, 1996.

marriage contributes to the recruitment process. We define pornography broadly to include not only traditional forms such as "men's" magazines and X-rated videos (and now computer porn), but any sexually explicit material which promotes sex outside of marriage, including many broadcast and cable television programs, certain "women's" magazines (the ones which are emblazoned with lurid sexual messages at supermarket check-out lines), and, of course, many Hollywood movies of various ratings. Parents who openly bring pornography in any form into their home send a silent message to their child that sexual behavior outside of marriage is normal and acceptable. This lowers a child's motivation and ability to say "no" when an opportunity for sexual experimentation presents itself, *even if he or she is reluctant to experiment.* In fact, the child may think he is not normal (or like Dad) if he *doesn't* experiment. (It goes without saying that in our society, wherever there are opportunities for kids to have sex, opportunities for homosexual behavior will be among them.) It is a short journey from that attitude to active sexual experimentation of various sorts, including homosexual experimentation.

Monkey See, Monkey Do

Aside from any intellectual conclusions which a child may draw from his parent's tacit approval of pornography, the child may begin to use pornography himself, simply because it is available in his home. Such children are much more seriously endangered for several reasons. For one thing, a child or teenager who is already indoctrinated into the excesses and dehumanizing attitudes of pornography has already been "set up" as a victim (or worse, as a victimizer). His threshold of tolerance for sexual aggression is now very high. According to their testimonies, many young victims of homosexual molestation were shown pornography by their molesters as an introductory tactic. And all pornography has homosexual elements. Even so-called "soft-core" porn promotes homosexuality and the "gay" mind-set, while hard-core porn encompasses every imaginable perversion. Family issues

Seven Steps to Recruit-Proof Your Child

155

researcher, Dr. Judith Reisman, has suggested that pornography use is itself a type of homosexuality since the typical chain of supply and demand consists of men (porn producers and distributors) providing other men (consumers) with sexual stimulation. In any case, pornography can itself be as addictive as homosexual behavior and should be kept far away from children.

Internet -- the Techno-Trojan Horse

A special danger which has arisen with the computer revolution is the Internet. The Internet is to computer technology what the American West was to pioneering in the last century: it is wild, raw and unpredictable. However, unlike the old West, the Internet frontier is available to children of any age from the comfort of their own homes, as well as from many schools and public libraries. A child with basic computer skills and Internet access can gain entry to any of literally hundreds of pornographic websites with a few simple keystrokes. What is more, the child needn't search for such material; many unscrupulous porn vendors send unsolicited e-mail invitations to family homes, complete with links to pornographic web sites which will open at the click of a button. Many of these sites claim to restrict access to adult members, but most offer samples of their wares for any Internet visitor to view, usually ultra-hardcore porn photos, including graphic homosexual scenes.

The "gay" movement has taken full advantage of the Internet to gain access to young people. Literally thousands of homosexual sites are on-line, many of which are also linked to porn vendors. The most threatening sites, however, are those of supposedly reputable organizations like Planned Parenthood, which lure young people with the promise of "family planning" advice, but which provide direct links to a number of homosexual web sites which in turn are directly or indirectly linked to porn vendors and to pornographic web sites of other "gay" groups. Many young people have been recruited into homosexuality on the Internet, often by adult predators posing as fellow teens.

We encourage parents to carefully monitor their child's

"GAY" HEROES

"Make gays look good. In order to make a Gay Victim sympathetic to straights you have to portray him as Everyman. But an additional theme of the campaign should be more aggressive and upbeat...the campaign should paint gays as *superior* pillars of society. Yes, yes, we know -- this trick is so old it creaks....In no time, a skillful and clever media campaign could have the gay community looking like the veritable fairy godmother to Western Civilization."

Marshall Kirk and Erastus Pill, "The Overhauling of Straight America," *Guide Magazine*, November 1987.

"Homosexual rights activists point to lesbians and homosexual men who are talented, educated, courageous, famous, or accomplished in many fields and assert that these and similar admirable qualities entitle them to civil rights protections for their sexual practices. On the contrary, if the law wants to consider special civil rights status for such people, it should do so on the basis of their talent, education, courage, fame or accomplishments and not on the grounds of their sexual conduct. The brilliant writing of Dylan Thomas [an alcoholic], for example, might, if anything, encourage laws for the protection of poets, but not laws for the protection of drunkards."

David Llewellyn, "Logical Opposition To Homosexual Rights," *Life & Liberty*, 1994.

Internet usage and to avail themselves of one of the many "blocking" programs which have become available to prevent access to harmful sites. A parent's best defense, however, will be his child's own self-restraint and judgment. The safest child in any dangerous or entrapping situation is the child whose home training has given him clear moral guidelines and the ability to reason soundly.

No Practicing "Gay" Role Models

A child should not be forced into a situation where his love and respect for a role model could be used to gain his acceptance of the homosexual lifestyle. In fact "gay" teachers have been encouraged by "gay" activists to "come out" to their students in the classroom for this very purpose. The best approach a parent can take is to maintain a policy of not allowing a child to come under the direct influence of any openly homosexual role model, even if the person does not appear to be a potential sexual predator. This policy should even include relatives who are not actively seeking help for their condition. The influence of homosexuals in the arts and popular culture poses a different problem. Such people are not true role models but can often influence young minds. Indeed, the "gay" movement points to famous "gays" in history and in our contemporary culture in their campaign to legitimize homosexual behavior. They imply that homosexuality must be normal if such and such great artist or statesman was "gay." A parent might wish to point out that artistic talent or high achievement does not validate a person's private lifestyle, whether it be homosexuality, drug addiction or any other destructive behavior.

We should also mention that many of the historical figures touted as "gay" by zealous homosexual activists were probably not homosexual. Bear in mind that some "gay historians" have claimed Abraham Lincoln and Jesus as their own.

Gay rights are now a key factor in city contracts

■ Contractors that allow discrimination against gays lesbians no longer may pro and services to Portland

By MICHELE PARENTE
of The Oregonian staff

The Portland City Cou considerable financia Wednesday by banning b out a formal gay rights tracting with the city.
The ban affects city 3,000 businesses a year $200 million in goods rule is believed to be ment policy of its kind
In a combined un council also set up tion program to he discrimination prot landmark civil rig law, which prohib the basis of sexua ing and employm

City and County
of San Francisco
Human Rights Commission

Affirmative Action:

How it Benefits
Lesbian Gay Bisexual
Transgender People

"America in the 1990s is the time and place for rage — ice-cold, controlled, directed rage."

Marshall Kirk and Hunter Madsen, *After the Ball*, p. 382, 1990.

"I can envision a day when straight people say, 'So what if you're promoting homosexuality.'"

Kevin Jennings, Executive Director, Gay, Lesbian and Straight Education Network (GLSEN), quoted in the *Lambda Report*, Jan/Feb 1998.

Step Seven

Be Active in Your Community

The Importance of Community Involvement

While a healthy, family-centered home provides the best protection against "gay" recruitment of children, it is not in itself a complete defense. The larger community also influences a child's choices and attitudes. A parent's efforts on behalf of his child should include efforts to make his community more family-friendly. Indeed, the need for such involvement has become critical.

Law and public policy in our system of government is heavily influenced by public debate (often highly emotional and divisive) among those with competing ideas and philosophies. For good or ill, those who are hesitant or unwilling to promote and defend their ideas and interests are the inevitable losers in such a system. Parents must realize that reluctance to speak out on behalf of their children, especially on controversial issues such as homosexuality, grants a certain amount of control over their children's future to others. In today's political climate, those "others" include highly organized

1972 GAY RIGHTS PLATFORM

1. Elimination of bars to the entry...and naturalization of ["gay"] aliens.

2. **Encouragement and support for sex education courses, prepared and taught by gay men and women, presenting homosexuality as a valid, healthy preference and lifestyle as a viable alternative to heterosexuality.**

3. Regulations and legislation banning the compiling, maintenance and dissemination of information on an individual's sexual preferences...

4. [Public] funding of all programs of gay men's and women's organizations designed to alleviate [discrimination]...

5. Immediate release of all gay men and women now incarcerated in ...prisons and mental institutions because of sexual offense[s]...

6. Repeal of all state laws prohibiting private sexual acts involving consenting persons; equalization for homosexuals and heterosexuals for the enforcement of laws.

7. Repeal of all state laws prohibiting solicitation for private voluntary sexual liaisons; and laws [banning] **prostitution**, both male and female.

8. Enactment of legislation prohibiting insurance companies and any other state regulated enterprises from discriminating ...

9. Enactment of legislation so that **child custody, adoption, visitation rights, foster parenting**, and the like shall not be denied because of sexual orientation or marital status.

10. Repeal all laws prohibiting transvestitism and cross-dressing.

11. **Repeal all laws governing age of sexual consent.**

12. Repeal all legislative provisions that restrict the **sex or number** of persons entering into a marriage unit; and the extension of legal benefits to all persons who cohabit regardless of sex or numbers.

National Coalition of Gay Organizations, Chicago, February 1992.

161

and dedicated "gay" activists. What is more, parents can no longer assume that their interests will be represented by other family-minded people. In past years when family values were more commonplace, parents could afford to "let the other guy do it," but not today. So many family-minded people have opted to "let the other guy do it" that there just aren't many "other guys" to "do it" any more. Parents must begin to take an active role in shaping the policies of their communities.

Get the Facts Before You Act

Unfortunately, in today's "politically correct" climate, a parent's pro-family efforts will not go unchallenged. Simply by standing up for traditional family values, a parent will be perceived by homosexualists as a political enemy to be defeated. What is more, the "gay" movement is not only very experienced at dealing with parents, but it is deeply entrenched in the power structure of many state and local governments and has strategies and mechanisms already in place to counter any opposition to its agenda. It is best, therefore, to proceed cautiously. Take the time to learn about the homosexual political agenda and its means of implementation. You will find that the larger part of this chapter is devoted to discussing the "gay" agenda, because effective parental response requires an awareness of how far this agenda has progressed in the local community.

The "Gay" Agenda

Homosexualists usually affect puzzlement at the mention of a "gay" agenda. "What gay agenda?" they say. "Gays and lesbians only want what everyone else wants: equal rights and the chance to live their lives as who they are." The assertion that homosexuals only want equal rights is itself a calculated response, part of the tactics commonly used to further the "gay" agenda. Perhaps more than any other political activists, "gays" are thoroughly versed in the radical doctrines and goals of their cause. In this section we will

"GAY" AGENDA? WHAT "GAY" AGENDA?

"Breaking the sexual taboo agreement has serious consequences. For gay people there is no choice...There is no right or wrong about sex, only problems of self-esteem and community survival."

The Advocate, June 12, 1980.

"In the end, the gay alternative means a departure not just from heterosexuality but from social orthodoxy...Gay liberation is a social event. In its most moderate politics — the enactment of civil rights legislation — it has radical value because civil rights legislation means the way to acceptance and acceptance means the way to dissolution of the norm."

Homosexualist Richard Goldstein in the *Village Voice*, June 24, 1984.

"Feminism, technology, and transgenderism have debunked the myth of a 'male and female world.' Life has much more gender potential than we can imagine. As we break free of the chains of sexual apartheid, we will establish a new human culture of unparalled creativity....From *Homo sapiens*, literally the 'wise man,' shall emerge our new species, *Persona creatas*, the 'creative person.'"

Martine Roseblatt, *The Apartheid of Sex: A Manifesto on the Freedom of Gender*. In *Lambda Report*, July-September 1995.

examine the goals of the "gay" movement as well as the strategies and tactics which it employs in pursuit of them. This information is valuable for parents who want to understand how to recognize "gay" political maneuvering in their own communities.

"GAY" GOALS

The primary goal of the "gay" movement is to gain the political power to force acceptance of homosexuality upon all of society, including the power to punish dissenters. (This last point of the "gay" agenda can be seen in the heavy-handed use of authority to punish failure to go along with pro-"gay" policies in "politically correct" environments, and from the "gay" movement's history of relentless vilification of its adversaries.) The implications of this statement, however, may not be apparent unless we consider the fact that the "gay" philosophy of unrestricted sexual license is diametrically opposed to the Judeo-Christian sexual ethic which has held sway in this country from its beginnings. These two philosophies are utterly incompatible and irreconcilable. For the "gay" philosophy to prevail, the Judeo-Christian philosophy must fail; they cannot coexist because their beliefs and goals are mutually exclusive. Parents must fully appreciate this one important fact in order to understand why the "gay" movement is such a destructive force in our society.

The greatest danger of the "gay" movement does *not* lie in any single agenda item, such as "gay" marriage or anti-discrimination statutes, or even from the "gay" movement's campaign to recruit children. The "gay" movement's greatest threat to society arises from its fundamental and necessary goal: to eliminate the Judeo-Christian sexual ethic (monogamous, heterosexual, family-centered marriage) as the guiding moral standard for sexual behavior in our culture. Judeo-Christian sexual morality unequivocally condemns homosexuality. Therefore, to gain a status of legitimacy for their lifestyle, "gay" activists must put an end to society's commitment to the traditional husband-wife relationship in the nuclear family. In its place, they must promote an alternative

MUDDYING THE MORAL WATERS

"While public opinion is one primary source of mainstream values, religious authority is the other. When conservative churches condemn gays, there are only two things we can do to confound the homophobia of true believers. First, we can use talk to muddy the moral waters. This means publicizing support for gays by more moderate churches, raising theological objections of our own about conservative interpretations of biblical teachings, and exposing hatred and inconsistency. Second, we can undermine the moral authority of homophobic churches by portraying them as antiquated backwaters, badly out of step with the times and with the latest findings of psychology. Against the mighty pull of institutional Religion one must set the mightier draw of Science and Public Opinion (the shield and sword of that accursed 'secular humanism'). Such an unholy alliance has worked well against churches before, on such topics as divorce and abortion. With enough open *talk* about the prevalence and acceptability of homosexuality, that alliance can work again here."

Marshall K. Kirk & Erastes Pill, "The Overhauling of Straight America," *Guide Magazine*, November 1987.

sexual paradigm which embraces homosexuality and other wholly non-procreative forms of sexual expression. In short, the goal of the "gay" movement is to remake society in its own image.

"GAY" STRATEGIES

Denormalize Heterosexual Monogamy

Since the rise of the American "gay" movement in the 1940s, "gay" activists have pursued several consistent strategies. One strategy is to de-normalize heterosexual monogamy and normalize sexual deviance through the release of highly-publicized, controversial findings of "junk" science. The first and most explosive of such efforts was the famous study of the sexual behavior of American men, published by Alfred Kinsey in 1948. The Kinsey Report instantly shocked and scandalized the nation. It was acclaimed, however, by academics and eventually served as a launch pad for the so-called sexual revolution. Kinsey's study purported to show that, despite appearances to the contrary, high percentages of Americans were living secret lives of marital infidelity and engaging in sexual deviance of every sort. Most Americans weren't living such lives in 1948, but Kinsey himself was. Only recently it has been acknowledged by his former associates that Kinsey (now deceased) was an "in the closet" homosexual activist and sexual libertine who produced fraudulent statistics for the purpose of reshaping American attitudes about sexual deviance. Kinsey's faked results yielded several enduring "gay"-positive myths, including the still widely quoted statistic that ten percent of the population is homosexual (several recent studies place the figure at around two percent). Kinsey also gets the credit for popularizing the view, now widely promoted by top U.S. sex researchers and many academics, that all types of sexual expression are equal (even sex with children and animals) when you take away society's "artificial" moral limits.

A "gay" youth organization protests at a pro-life event.

POST-KINSEYAN CHANGES IN SEX LAWS
AND THEIR IMPACT ON MARRIAGE

"[The de-sanctification of marriage led to the decriminalization of 'seduction' and 'breach of promise' to marry] These new law [codes], of course, required that both contraception and abortion become legally destigmatized and widely available to unmarried females. Once this occurred, women became the consenting 'partner' responsible for both creating and ending a baby's life. Previously, the man was held legally and socially responsible for creating the life and no one was allowed to end it. Under the new laws, women's rights were offset by men's freedoms and women's new burdens. A result anticipated by many early feminist reformers such as Susan B. Anthony, who were strongly pro-marriage and anti-abortion."

Judith A. Reisman, Ph..D. *KINSEY: Crimes & Consequences*. p. 243, 1998.

Be Active In Your Community

Pornography

Another strategy of the "gay" movement is to promote activities and choices which corrupt the sexual morals of the heterosexual majority. The pornography industry, for example, ostensibly caters to a demand for its product among heterosexual men. The success of the industry, however, serves the "gay" cause, since any man who permits himself the indulgence of pornography is probably going to be unwilling to condemn homosexual practices on moral grounds. Such a man is even less likely to *publicly* oppose the "gay" agenda, since he will already have a personal investment in the protection of a class of behavior which society has traditionally repudiated.

Abortion

"Abortion rights" is another social issue championed by "gays." Observers of the abortion issue often question why both male and female homosexuals often dominate the pro-abortion side at abortion-related events. After all, unplanned pregnancy is not likely to be a problem in a homosexual relationship! It is sometimes assumed that female homosexuals are altruistically taking up the cause of their heterosexual "sisters" on this issue, but "gay" interest in promoting abortion is not motivated by altruism but by self-interest. The existence of a thriving abortion industry profoundly benefits the "gay" cause in the same manner that the porn trade does: it corrupts and silences people who might otherwise oppose the "gay" agenda. In addition, every choice for abortion is itself a validation of the self-centered "gay" philosophy of sexual freedom without consequences. Abortion lends much credence to the idea of human ability to "design" or control the form and function of the natural family unit. Just as homosexuals desire to shape artificial family units by combining persons without natural ties, so they are attracted to the idea of dismantling the natural family by eliminating one or more of its members and thus altering the roles and relationships of the rest.

168

"A federal judge refused to remove a photo exhibit of homosexual households from elementary schools in Amherst, Massachusetts...The 20 black and white photos, titled 'Love Makes a Family: Living in Gay and Lesbian Families,' depict children with their homosexual parents. Three women who organized the show said the photos were designed to 'address issues of family diversity and homophobia.'"

National and International Religion Report, May 27, 1996.

"On May 28 CBS re-ran an hour-long afternoon TV special aimed at convincing viewers that homosexual couples are an equal substitute for mom and dad in parenting children. *Other Mothers*...is part of the 'CBS Schoolbreak Special'...[for] school-age children...The attractive, intelligent, sensitive lesbians are contrasted with the bigoted, paranoid community homophobes."

AFA Journal, August 1996.

Redefining the Family

The promotion of a new concept of family which does away with any requirement for a legal or common law heterosexual marriage has recently become a *cause celebre* for homosexual activists. Partly to validate such a concept, homosexuals have demanded and received adoption rights in several states and formed domestic groups which they portray as examples of successful "nontraditional families." A lesbian organization in Oregon which promotes this concept has a name which is also its marketing slogan: "Love Makes a Family." Implicit in such promotion is the notion that family is not a real social entity but a construct of the human imagination, in this case guided by nothing more binding than emotion. It has been pointed out that this kind of thinking leads logically to a situation in which society would have to grant family status to every imaginable conglomeration of people with fond feelings for one another. Thus, if society had no right to deny two homosexuals and an adopted child the designation and legal status of a family, what right could it have to deny such a designation to three homosexuals and a child? Or any other size and type of group? The redefined family unit would have no societal significance (other than a legal one) and no necessary social functions at all.

Pro-"Gay" Indoctrination

One other strategy which was only made possible by previous political gains is the strategy of reshaping social attitudes, especially those of children and young people, through indoctrination. Indoctrination of children occurs primarily through pro-"gay" advocacy in the schools and through the entertainment media. The effect of a pan-societal homosexual propaganda campaign which reaches parents and other adults, is to reap additional benefits for the "gay" movement in the form of a more sympathetic public. The pervasiveness of "politically correct" attitudes among the media and cultural elites (aside from modeling such attitudes for children) also leads many people to conclude that society as a whole has

DEMANDS OF THE 1993 "GAY" MARCH ON WASHINGTON

1. We demand passage of a Lesbian, Gay, Bisexual, and Transgender civil rights bill and an end to discrimination by state and federal governments including the military; repeal of all sodomy laws and other laws that criminalize private sexual expression between consenting adults.

2. We demand massive increase funding for AIDS education, research, and patient care; universal access to health care including alternative therapies; and an end to sexism in medical research and health care.

3. We demand legislation to prevent discrimination against Lesbians, Gays, Bisexuals and Transgendered people in the areas of family diversity, custody, adoption and foster care and that the definition of family includes the full diversity of all family structures.

4. We demand full and equal inclusion of Lesbians, Gays, Bisexuals and Transgendered people in the educational system, and inclusion of Lesbian, Gay, Bisexual and Transgender studies in multicultural curricula.

5. We demand the right to reproductive freedom and choice, to control our own bodies, and an end to sexist discrimination.

6. We demand an end to racial and ethnic discrimination in all forms.

7. We demand an end to discrimination and violent oppression based on actual or perceived sexual orientation/identification, race, religion, identity, sex and gender expression, disability, age, class, AIDS/HIV infection.

accepted the idea that being "gay" is normal.

We hope that parents will perceive that the promotion of the "gay" agenda by homosexual activists directly threatens their children. This part of the book has been about issues and policies which are abroad in the society, each one which relates to the society's moral health and the social climate in which our children spend their days. Each parent must confront and understand these issues, the state of our culture, and where it may be headed, to properly steer his or her child away from specific harmful situations.

"GAY" TACTICS

We now turn from the various strategies of homosexual activists to the tactics used to carry them out. The "gay" movement employs many and varied tactics in the implementation of its strategies. Such tactics commonly fall into three general categories: political, sociological and psychological.

POLITICAL TACTICS

By political tactics we mean the organized advancement of "gay" strategies through traditional political means: statutes, lawsuits, lobbying and so on. Players in every sector of the modern political arena seem to have adopted the attitude that "all's fair in love and war" and concluded that politics is outright war. Motivated by a deep resentment of the status quo, and driven to overcome their outsider status, the activists of the "gay" movement have adopted a no-holds-barred warrior mentality; they are among the most cunning and relentless fighters on the battlefield. A long and impressive string of victories bears testimony to their effectiveness. For parents concerned about the safety and health of their children, however, the militancy and dedication of "gay" political activists present a tremendous challenge.

SILENCING DISSENT

"The homosexual agenda was flying high at the Federal Aviation Administration (FAA), Department of Commerce (DOC) and the Environmental Protection Agency (EPA) in June with the agencies celebrating June's Gay Pride Month. All 45,000 FAA employees were encouraged to appreciate the positive aspects of the homosexual lifestyle. Opportunities to take part in Gay Pride Month activities were supposedly strictly voluntary but workers were led to believe those objecting to the gay events would be punished. To illustrate the fact, attendance to one event was billed as not being mandatory but for an unspecified reason, a list of those who chose to attend was kept."

Clarion-Ledger, June 13, 1996

"We should have shut down the subway and burned down city hall. I think rioting is a valid tactic and should be tried...If someone took out [killed] Jesse Helms or William Dannemeyer of California, I would be the first to stand up and applaud."

ACT-UP member Michael Petrelis, quoted in Michael Wilrich. "Uncivil Disobedience." *Mother Jones*, p. 16, December 1990.

Intimidation

It is true that, "gay" political victories have not, to this point, reflected the will of the people. Parents who desire to shield their children from pressure to accept homosexuality as normal should not take such victories as a sign that they are standing alone against a completely pro-"gay" population. Most people still disapprove of the "gay" lifestyle and continue to express concerns about the "gay" political agenda. "Gay" victories have been won *despite* public disapproval, primarily because most of the critical battles on homosexual issues are won behind the scenes, often by the use of intimidation and harassment — not because public opinion favors the "gay" position on the issue. We are not suggesting that "gay" activists are alone in employing such tactics, just that, in the absence of popular support, they have become especially adept at using them. One of the reasons for continued "gay" political success is that there are no adversaries with a great enough stake in the issue to counter aggressively unprincipled, often vicious and personal, tactics.

Tactics of harassment and intimidation are especially effective in small-scale battles outside of the public view, in which none of the key decision-makers have the public stature to single-handedly rally public opinion to their defense. The takeover of the American Psychiatric Association by homosexualists in 1973 is a prime example of such a battle. The majority of psychiatrists opposed a policy of normalizing homosexuality, but a vote-by-mail decision was organized and funded by "gay" activists, who carefully controlled the mailing list. Opponents were kept disorganized and defensive by "gay" activists who heckled them at scientific conferences and public appearances and began referring to them publicly as "war criminals" (with obvious implications). The easy conquest of the APA on this important clinical policy (which should have been decided by scientific inquiry, not a *vote*) exposed the weakness of such organizations, which the "gay" movement proceeded to exploit very successfully elsewhere. Small democratically-run organizations are often vulnerable to takeover

174

"SECRET AGENTS"

"Being a married bisexual also gives me a certain responsibility and freedom. I can educate in ways someone who is not in a 'conventional' relationship cannot. I can bring up issues of homophobia, biphobia, and AIDS without fearing that I will be labeled or ostracized. I can question those who express prejudice or intolerance with impunity. And I do. Since I am a teacher, this role of educator is especially important to me....I know I walk a fine line when I question students' phobic beliefs. Many of these students' parents are homophobic and racist, and the students mimic their parent's values. Yet my job is to get them to think about their assumptions and to make their own decisions. I also know that if I were open about my sexuality I might be fired or harassed. So in my work I am closeted, cloaked by my seemingly traditional marriage. I found I have to choose my battles and then fight them with fierce determination."

Amanda Yoshizaki, "I am who I am -- A married bisexual teacher," in Loraine Hutchins and Lani Kaahumanu (eds.), *Bi Any Other Name: Bisexual People Speak Out*, 1991.

"We Are Everywhere"

Popular "gay" bumper sticker.

by well-organized special interest groups. This brings us to a social characteristic of the "gay" community which has given its members a natural advantage in the infiltration of hostile organizations.

Deception

"Gay" activists have a unique tradition of covert political tactics because of the nature of the "gay" lifestyle. Active but covert ("in the closet") homosexuals have always had to deceive their closest non-"gay" associates to protect themselves from disclosure. Indeed, the "gay" lifestyle has been characterized by secrecy and deception. At the same time, the bonds of loyalty and commonality which develop between homosexuals who share this secret "gay" identity is understandably very powerful. "In the closet" homosexuals, therefore, are both positioned and predisposed to function cooperatively and covertly in organizations of which they are members. This situation is exemplified by the "old-boy" networks in some corporations and bureaucratic agencies which have very high percentages of "gay" employees. "Gays" influence the hiring of more "gays" and put pressure on the organization to bring about pro-"gay" policies, donations, etc. This system, when covert, also works against its members, making them vulnerable to blackmail and forcing their loyalty to a group whose interests may conflict with the organization's. For this reason, U.S. intelligence agencies had a policy of denying top-secret security clearance to homosexuals for many years. This policy was ended by President Clinton in 1992.

Opportunism

In recent years overt "gay" pressure groups have emerged in many of America's largest corporations, such as AT&T and Disney, using their power to exact privileges and benefits and to steer corporate funds and policies. Intra-organizational policy changes typically include "sensitivity training" for non-homosexual employees (see below). "Gay" influence in corporate relations with

ENGINEERING CHANGE

"Mr. Chiumento played an active role in attempting to include sexual orientation in his local union contract's nondiscrimination clause ('There's no cost, except the ink to print it,' he pointed out with the savvy of a union negotiator)....'We've got material from PFLAG, and a booklet we put together filled with information on bargaining language from around the U.S., and why sexual orientation should be included in every contract.'"

Dan Woog, *School's Out - The Impact of Gay and Lesbian Issues on America's Schools,* p. 286, 1995.

"Lesbian activists entered a Massachusetts elementary school on Valentine's Day and passed pro-homosexual leaflets that contained a toll-free number for 'Hot, Uncensored Gay Sex.' [T]he Lesbian Avengers, a militant lesbian group, [passed] out fliers that proclaimed: 'Girls Who Love Girls and Women Who Love Women are OK!!! Happy Valentine's Day.' Each leaflet had a piece of candy attached...The literature listed an 800-number for what it claimed was the 'National Lesbian and Gay Hotline.' But the Associated Press (AP) reported that callers got a recording advertising 'American's Wildest, Hottest Phone Sex Service.'

Lambda Report, Spring 1994.

the community can be seen in advertising themes, in political endorsements and contributions, in loans of executives to "gay" causes, in charitable giving and in the terms of collective bargaining agreements. Often "gay" control of a company's community relations assets is used to pressure other organizations. In the mid-1990s, Levi Strauss, Wells Fargo and Bank of America, for example, were part of a group of "gay"-influenced corporations which publicly criticized the Boy Scouts of America for refusing to allow homosexuals to be scout leaders.

"Gay" control of a single organization can accomplish much for the "gay" cause, but is even more powerful in influencing relations *between* organizations, say, in a contract negotiation between a public employees' union and a government agency. In practical political situations, the "gay" community wields power far greater than its numbers simply by having cooperating members in many organizations. One woman of our acquaintance was asked to be on a committee to help her city host a traveling Anne Frank exhibit; she was surprised by the heavy emphasis on homosexual victims of the Nazis which was proposed by members of the group. She was astonished to learn that the local "gay" community not only had representation on the committee in its own right, but that the representatives of several other groups, including a priest from the Episcopal church, were also homosexuals. She lost the vote on whether to include the homosexual emphasis, but learned an important lesson about "gay" politics.

SOCIOLOGICAL TACTICS

The "gay" movement also employs tactics of social engineering to achieve political ends. Social engineering is the process of steering social change by the manipulation of public attitudes and behaviors. "Gay"-related social engineering works to legitimize homosexuality in our society primarily by appealing to our children (a strategy which looks ahead to the future), but also by shaping the opinions of adults.

"RAINBOW" COALITIONS

"The gay community should join forces with other civil liberties groups of respectable cast to promote bland messages about America the Melting-Pot, always ending with an explicit reference to the [National Gay and Lesbian] Task Force or some other gay organization. ...Our next indirect step will be to advertise locally on behalf of support groups *peripheral* to the gay community: frowzy straight moms and dads announcing phone numbers and meeting times for "Parents of Gays" or similar gatherings. Can't you just see such ads now, presented between messages from the Disabled Vets and the Postal Worker's Union?"

Marshall K. Kirk & Erastes Pill, "The Overhauling of Straight America," *Guide Magazine*, November 1987.

"At least one of the nation's black newspapers already has a regular column written by an avowed and uncloseted homosexual. Another introduces 'positive' images of homosexuals on its children's pages. As would be expected, the black elite, so adept at aping the worst behaviors of white society, has already opened doors to the further dissemination of homosexual propaganda and images in the black community. Such people have so tightly forged the link between African-American and homosexual activists that a teacher's periodical entitled *Interracial Books for Children* devotes an entire issue to promoting homosexual books for *guess whose children*?"

Unidentified black commentator, *Issues and Views*, Fall 1992 (emphasis in original).

"Bundling"

The "gay" movement's key to manipulating public attitudes about homosexuality in America today is the concept of civil rights. The "gay" civil rights strategy exploits disorganization or disunity among legitimate minorities to gain power in local civil rights coalitions; the civil rights groups can then be pressured to "bundle" homosexuals together with less powerful ethnic and racial groups, giving homosexuals the appearance of having both biological standing and a socially disadvantaged status. Such coalitions (often controlled by "gay" money and leaders but usually headed by a minority spokesperson), will then speak on behalf of the homosexual cause in any setting in which effective opposition to "gay rights" might slow or halt the advance of the "gay" agenda. This tactic of "bundling" themselves into coalitions with minorities exploits the public's disapproval of racism (and individuals' fear of being called racist) to shield homosexuals from the scrutiny and criticism which "gay" activists would otherwise certainly receive.

Human Rights Commissions

A typical vehicle for the "bundling" tactic is the local human rights commission. The human rights commission is tailor-made for advancing homosexual goals in any local community; the concept may in fact have been specifically developed by the "gay" movement. Human rights commissions are quasi-governmental or governmental agencies which have been springing up in cities around the nation in increasing numbers in recent years. The establishment of human rights commissions has followed a similar sequence of events in several cities. First, there will be stories or editorials in the local news media on "hate crimes" against racial minorities. Next, apparently in response to the "hate crimes," comes a proposal and vote in the city council to create an organization (staffed by minority leaders) to monitor human rights abuses in the community. The new commission usually receives government office space and tax funding to carry on its work, although members

PHONY HATE CRIMES

South Carolina lesbian charged with staging pair of beatings

CRIME: Regan Wolf's claims renewed calls for a hate-crime law; police say she paid attackers.

By KIM CURTIS
The Associated Press

LANCASTER, S.C. — A lesbian whose claim that she was twice beaten by an intruder at her home renewed calls for a hate-crime law in South Carolina was charged Wednesday with staging both incidents. Investigators said Regan Wolf, 40, even offered a friend $250 to administer one of the beatings. Wolf surrendered to authorities Wednesday and was released for a court appearance July 28. If convicted of giving false information to a law enforcement officer, she could get a month in jail and a $200 fine. A scraped and bruised Wolf had claimed that she was twice beaten and tied up. State Sen. Darrell Jackson used her story to...

National News Briefs

Authorities Say Lesbian Staged Her Two Beatings

LANCASTER, S.C., July 15 (AP) — Regan Wolf, a lesbian whose claim ... Ms. Wolf surrendered today was released for a court appearance on July 28. If convicted of giving information to a law-enforcement officer, she could be sentenced month in jail.

"In the City of Eugene, businesses that had supported the Oregon Citizens Alliance (which had sponsored the ballot initiative) had bricks, wrapped in swastika-embellished flyers, thrown through their windows....[An] organization which called itself 'Bigot Busters' specialized in harassing and threatening petitioners seeking signatures to put the measure on the ballot. Petitions were ripped from circulators hands or doused with paint, activists blockaded petition tables, and several circulators were physically assaulted....Oregon homosexual activists cast themselves as victims during this campaign of violence. A series of phony late-night cross-burnings were staged in the front yard of Azalea Cooley, a black, apparently wheelchair-bound lesbian in Portland. This highly publicized charade continued for six months and was blamed on a "climate of hate" created by OCA. On the eve of the election, however, police caught Cooley herself on video *walking* out her own front door with a wooden cross and materials to burn it. She later confessed to all of the crimes (*Oregonian*, December 10, 1992).

Scott Lively and Kevin Abrams, *The Pink Swastika: Homosexuality in the Nazi Party*, pp. 206-207, 1997.

of the commission are usually not paid. Typically, one of the organization's first acts is to propose a new law (which is always enacted) banning discrimination based on race, religion, ethnic group, and so on. If the words "sexual orientation" are not included in the list at first, they are usually added later. And, invariably, open homosexuals representing the local "gay" community are given one or more positions on the commission. (The community never learns whether or how many representatives of other groups on the commission are actually "in the closet" homosexuals.)

Once a human rights commission begins operating in a local community, the "gay" community gains official government validation of the "gay" claim of minority status just by holding seats on the commission. Further, the resources and assets of the commission, including its taxpayer-funded budget, can be used to advance other "gay" strategies. For example, human rights commissions issue regular reports on "hate crimes" in the local community, broken down by the type of victim, including a category for homosexuals. The timing and emphasis of such reports can have a significant impact on public opinion; this has been the case during at least some of the political initiatives to limit "gay rights" legislation in various parts of the country. Inflated "hate crimes" statistics were published in these communities to suggest that local opposition to "gay" plans and activities causes an increase in violence against homosexuals. Human rights commission "gay"-related "hate crimes" statistics put out during such times are usually meaningless, since they include such things as unsubstantiated telephone complaints which could easily be part of a political "phone-in" campaign (a favorite tactic of "gay" activist organizations).

Exploiting Civil Rights Weaknesses

"Gay" claims of minority status bring uncertainty and confusion to civil rights laws and doctrines. Two of the most basic criteria which justify granting special status and benefits to minorities are economic disadvantage and lack of political power.

CIVIL RIGHTS FOR HOMOSEXUALITY?

"Homosexuality, or sexual orientation, is a descriptive status based upon conduct. Conduct, including sexual conduct, has always been subject to legal regulation in the public interest. On the contrary, personal characteristics, not conduct, have always been the basis for civil rights. The contorted attempts by homosexual rights advocates to claim that people are entitled to civil rights protection for their sexual orientation without regard to their conduct simply underscores the foundational error of the homosexuals' claim. *Homosexuals are not claiming a right to be eunuchs. They are demanding legal protection to engage in homosexual practices without legal repercussions* ....Homosexuals claim that they are a minority subjected to discrimination, just like racial minorities. This analogy is false.

First, a person's race is determined at birth and established for life. It is a personal characteristic, not based upon conduct.

Second, racial prejudice is real prejudice, an irrational attitude insupportable by facts or logical argument. Race is a morally neutral characteristic, hence negative attitudes based solely on race are morally indefensible. Homosexual practices are not morally neutral to most people, hence negative attitudes based on homosexual practices are morally defensible.

Third, racist attitudes and homosexual behavior are judged by different moral standards. Homosexuals claim that homosexual conduct is morally neutral so long as people consent to engage in homosexual activity. Indeed, homosexual behavior is still a crime unless it is engaged in by consenting adults. Racism, on the other hand, is always morally evil and legally wrong. Racism could not be made morally or legally acceptable even if people were to consent to it.

Civil rights lawyer and constitutional law scholar, David Llewellyn, "Logical Opposition To Homosexual Rights," *Life & Liberty, 1994.* [Emphasis ours.]

Homosexuals cannot claim either of these conditions. Statistically, homosexuals enjoy significantly higher incomes than most Americans and their political lobby is among the most powerful in the nation. But "gay" claims for minority status founder before a more practical problem: homosexual applicants for minority benefits such as affirmative action cannot even prove that they are "gay." According to sexual orientation theory, *only the person asserting the claim* can know if he or she is "gay;" the criteria are purely subjective. This situation would allow *anyone* to collect *any* minority benefit just by claiming to be "gay." The stigma of homosexuality might prevent many people from saying they were "gay" (unless applications for benefits were confidential), but what about the rest who have been persuaded by the "gay" movement that "gay" is normal? Doesn't that number grow daily through the efforts of the "gay" movement itself? There is no way to limit or validate benefits granted to people on the basis of homosexual minority status.

The result of such an obvious invitation to commit fraud with impunity would be a loss of public confidence in *all* civil rights doctrines and programs (indeed this might be a factor in recent setbacks for affirmative action policies around the nation). Who loses in such a scenario? Not "gay" activists. They have the money and the power to advance their agenda by other means. The losers are the genuine minorities who have few other means available to them (the original reason for civil rights laws).

Bait and Switch

Another, and perhaps more damaging result of granting minority status to homosexuals is that civil rights protections and benefits do not just protect and benefit the *right to believe* one is "gay" as is implied by the use of the term "sexual orientation." Ironically, even though "sexual orientation" is supposedly a state of mind not defined by sexual behavior, the real effect of granting official minority status to homosexuals is to legitimize "gay" sex acts and to award legal and social benefits simply for the practice of

The Propaganda

IF YOU GO OUT OF YOUR WAY
TO PICK ON GAYS,
PSYCHIATRISTS HAVE A NAME FOR YOU.

... LATENT HOMOSEXUAL.

There was a time, years ago, when people
could hide their own homosexual tendencies
by loudly attacking other gays in public.

But not anymore.
These days, when you harass gay people,
it just puts the spotlight of suspicion on

So maybe you'd better mind your own b
unless you want others to think th
homosexuality is your business

A Message From   GAY AND L

THE
FACE
OF
BIGOTRY

Another victim of anti-gay violence

Sooner or later,
you'll have to face up to a choice—

Either you think this picture is okay or
you don't.

Either you make fun of 'fags' and 'dykes' or
you refuse to.

Either you hate gays, the same as bigots do,
or you say 'live and let live.'

So choose now.
Which kind of person do you want to be?

d of hating—that's what
bout.

ssage From
T NATIONAL GAY AND LESBIAN COMMUNITY

From *After the Ball*

**Survey: Gays victims
of domestic violence**

Gays and lesbians are more
likely to be the victims of domestic violence than anti-gay
violence but rarely report the
abuse, according
released Tuesday.

The National Co
Anti-Violence Pro
conducted the sur
results show that
relationships can
lent as heterosexu
ships sometimes a

The survey is b
scientific tabulati
acts of violence la
Chicago, Columbus, Ohio, Minneapolis, New York, San Diego
and San Francisco.

From Register news services

The Reality

"Gays and Lesbians
are more likely to be
victims of domestic
violence than anti-
gay violence but
rarely report the
abuse..."

185

them. How long can public confidence in civil rights laws be expected to last when such laws are viewed as "perks" for a type of sexual behavior? The public will have every reason to wonder what other behavior-based lifestyles will be next to gain minority status. It is inevitable that people will show a diminishing commitment to such an ill-founded system.

Victimology

The primary argument used by the "gay" movement to back its claim for "gay" minority status is that homosexuals have historically been victims of society's irrational prejudice, and that individual "gays" have been physically victimized because of this prejudice. It is true that some homosexuals have suffered violence at the hands of "gay-bashers," as they are called in the homosexual community. Such attacks, however, are less frequent than is suggested by the "gay" movement, and when such an incident occurs it may not be, as commonly alleged, an unprovoked assault by a heterosexual who hates homosexuals. Often homosexual "cruisers" ("gay"men who "cruise" public parks and restrooms looking for sex partners) are attacked in response to unwanted solicitations for "gay" sex. At other times a homosexual is beaten by his "gay" lover but is unwilling to implicate him ("gay" domestic violence rates are extremely high). Those responsible for unprovoked attacks on homosexuals may often be "latent" homosexuals themselves, or one of a type of ultra-masculine "gay" men (called "butches" in the homosexual jargon) who hate effeminate male "gays" ("femmes"). (Most attacks are against "femmes.") Many men who act out violent hostility towards homosexuals were themselves childhood victims of homosexual molestation. Such a motive does not in any sense excuse brutality against "gay" victims. Neither does the fact that "gays" have been mistreated legitimize "gay" behavior at all.

A tactic more reprehensible than exaggerating reports of "gay-bashings" is the exploitation of the Holocaust by the "gay" movement. "Gay" propagandists have fraudulently portrayed the internment of less than 15,000 homosexuals (in work camps, not

NONE DARE CALL IT BRAINWASHING

"Over at the Department of Commerce, Employees went through a month of 'Creating Common Ground' - a series of lectures designed to create a 'safer and more respectful workplace' for gay workers."

Clarion-Ledger, June 13, 1996.

"The Executive Team and CDC have determined that the first two priorities for Division-wide diversity training are racism and *heterosexism* [belief in the superiority of heterosexuality]. As you know, the first training has already occurred and the second is planned for this coming June. A staff survey has just been taken that provided valuable guidance for future training....Last, a few words on why our trainings require *mandatory attendance*. Our intent is to create a workplace climate that affirms respect for human diversity....It is <u>essential</u> that all Division staff be a part of the Division's agenda and change process. <u>Together</u>, we must learn. *<u>Together</u>, we must confront our fears and biases.* <u>Together</u>, we must grow.

From an employee memo, Multnomah County, Oregon, Department of Human Services, April 7, 1992. (Emphasis ours.)

death camps) by the Nazis as a "Gay Holocaust" equivalent to the attempted genocide of the Jews. "Gay" strategists have chosen the pink triangle (worn as an identification badge by homosexual prisoners) as the symbol of their movement, with the intention of forging a link between the plight of homosexuals and that of Jews in Nazi Germany. Similarly, opponents of so-called "gay-rights" are often portrayed as being like the Nazis to suggest that opposition to the "gay" cause is evil. Wherever there are Holocaust museums and educational projects, "gays" have secured places on boards and steering committees to ensure that the "gay" revision of Holocaust history gets wide public exposure. (One of the first people hired by the U.S. Holocaust Museum in Washington, D.C., the largest such museum in the world — was a "gay" activist whose duty it was to serve as liaison to the homosexual community). Conversely, homosexualist scholars have helped to suppress documentation of the central role which homosexuals played during the rise of the Nazi Party and throughout the Third Reich. (For a full discussion of this topic see *The Pink Swastika: Homosexuality in the Nazi Party* by Scott Lively and Kevin Abrams, Founders Publishing Corporation, Third Edition, 1997.)

PSYCHOLOGICAL TACTICS

Sensitivity Training

The psychological tactics used by the "gay" movement target individual subjects or groups rather than society as a whole. The most common such tactic is euphemistically called "sensitivity training." Sensitivity training is a system of mandatory moral re-education. Originally designed to reduce tensions between cultural groups in the workplace, it featured classes in which employees learned to appreciate the cultural customs and beliefs of their fellow workers. Workers attend classes together where they learn to appreciate the finer qualities of their fellow employees and their cultures. "Gay" sensitivity training uses the same group education format, but for the purpose of forcing acceptance of

188

GET THE CAMEL'S NOSE OUT OF THE TENT

"In the early stages of any campaign to reach straight America, the masses should not be shocked and repelled by premature exposure to homo*sexual* behavior itself. Instead, the imagery of sex should by downplayed and gay rights should be reduced to an abstract social question as much as possible. First let the camel get his nose inside the tent-and only later his unsightly derriere!"

Marshall K. Kirk & Erastes Pill, "The Overhauling of Straight America," *Guide Magazine*, November 1987.

"The campaign to teach schoolchildren that 'gay is O.K.' benefits from the usual coordination of a united 'gay' movement which has the advantage of pressing for a single radical goal, versus its pro-family opponents who face a multiplicity of challenges."

Peter LaBarbera, "'Homosexual Correctness' Advances in America's Schools." PNEWS Conferences, February 2, 1997.

"The teachers' unions, the National Education Association (NEA) and the California Teacher's Association (CTA), have produced a teacher training handbook: GAY AND LESBIAN YOUTH: BREAKING THE SILENCE...Children will be brainwashed right in the classroom unless parents...get districts to require that teachers not be allowed to promote homosexuality in the classroom."

Lou Sheldon, *Traditional Values Report*, Winter 1998.

homosexuality upon workers. Workers are required to attend one or more training sessions, often including visual images of homosexual contact of some sort, and are carefully observed for evidence of "homophobia" (any negative reaction to the notion that homosexuality is normal and good). Employees who have attended these sessions report being subjected to strong pressure to conform to the "politically correct" view, sometimes including veiled threats of reprisal for those who do not. "Gay" sensitivity training is now commonplace in corporate America, in many state and local government agencies, and everywhere in federal agencies under the Clinton administration.

Forewarned Is Forearmed

Our description of the "gay" agenda in America is by no means exhaustive, but should be sufficient to alert parents to the strong cultural pressures on their children. The most important fact to come away with is that the aggressive promotion of the "gay" movement is necessarily at cross-purposes with the vital function of the traditional family in American society. You must not underestimate the power and influence which this relatively small group wields. It is more than likely that you will encounter homosexual advocacy in your own or your child's environment, but if you understand the strategies and tactics of the "gay" movement, you can limit its effects.

What to Do About It

At this point in the process of recruit-proofing a child, a parent must decide how deeply he will get involved in opposing the homosexual agenda in his community. Some parents, upon discovering the true nature and the threat of the "gay" movement, become virtual family-protection crusaders. Others, recognizing the personal risk of standing up to homosexualists, look for ways to oppose the "gay" agenda indirectly or secretly. Most parents will choose a path somewhere between these two extremes. We suggest

TESTIMONIAL

"For most of my life, I was an openly gay man and a gay activist for six years. During those years, I had numerous intimate relationships, but in the late 1980s, after a suicide attempt, I was in utter despair. After completing nearly five years of gay-affirmative therapy, I came to the conclusion that homosexuality was the root of my loneliness and unhappiness. I wanted to find a way out, but was convinced that I was born gay by my gay therapist and the gay subculture. It's important to add that my depression was not a byproduct of societal homophobia. I found incredible acceptance and affirmation from my parents and family members. I found acceptance from a largely gay-affirmative environment. But I was, nonetheless, desperate for help. I sought out Christian-based counseling that unveiled environmental root causes to my homosexuality. With reparative therapy and a strong motivation to change, I overcame my homosexual orientation. Now, 10 years later, I have been happily married for five years. My first son, Timothy, is eight months old...The APA [American Psychiatric Association] is dead wrong in its unscientific assessment that efforts to change sexual orientation are potentially damaging. Many of my peers are celebrating the joy of new life after discovering that their homosexuality wasn't a biological imperative that they were doomed to follow."

Letter to the Editor by John Paulk, *Oregonian*, August 31, 1997.

three forms of activity, each of which will accommodate varying levels of personal involvement: pro-family political activism, nonpolitical family advocacy, and participating in ex-gay recovery efforts.

Pro-family Political Activism

There are many opportunities for parental involvement in pro-family political activism, from attending schoolboard or city council meetings to joining existing pro-family organizations. A few phone calls to local pro-family groups will be valuable in getting ideas. It is always best to spend some time to assess what is most needed at the present time before committing to any particular organization or effort. In such an information-gathering process, it helps to get to know school board members and other local political leaders to learn where they stand on the issues. Do this *before* you approach them with specific problems and you'll have a better chance to be listened to.

Get your information firsthand whenever possible. Remember, when it comes to any "politically correct" issue, *never* trust the news media's analysis or interpretation of events. Many great candidates and worthy campaigns have withered on the vine from lack of support or have been defeated at the polls because of the tendency of pro-family people to get their information from antifamily sources. In our opinion, more pro-family efforts are defeated by the combination of media misrepresentation and citizen gullibility than any other cause.

Pro-family activism includes both opposition to the bad and advocacy of the good. It is always helpful to offer an alternative when opposing a policy or proposal. For example, rather than simply voicing your concerns about a bad sex-ed curriculum, be prepared with information on abstinence-based programs or other alternatives. Additionally, involvement in the planning stages is better than showing up later to attack a completed plan.

STANDING UP FOR MORALITY
IS NOT POLITICAL

"The task of teaching moral literacy and forming character is not political in the usual meaning of the term. People of good character are not all going to come down on the same side of difficult political and social issues. Good people -- people of character and moral literacy -- can be conservative, and good people can be liberal. We must not permit our disputes over thorny political questions to obscure the obligation we have to offer instruction to all our young people in the area in which we have, as a society, reached a consensus: namely, on the importance of good character, and on some of its pervasive particulars."

William Bennett, *The Book of Virtues*, p. 13, 1993.

SIX STAGES OF DECISION MAKING

1. Identify the Problem
2. Analyze the Basic Issues
3. Identify the Possible Solutions
4. Establish the Criteria for Evaluating Solutions
5. Select Best Solution and Implement
6. Evaluate the Success of the Solution

From "Parent/Teen Communicator," *Sexuality Committment and Family*, p. 220, 1984.

Be Active In Your Community

Be proactive. A harmful trend among pro-family people is to fight only defensive battles. In other words, we wait for a problem to arise before we take action. This allows the "gay" movement to frame the issue in its own terms and to choose its own battles and battlefields. A better strategy is to assess the status of the local "gay" movement (based on what you have learned in this section) and to preempt the advancement of the "gay" agenda by placing a legislative or administrative roadblock in its way. For example, if the local government has not yet put an anti-discrimination policy in place, propose one that is limited to genuine minorities and requires a popular vote to change (however, never act alone in such a strategy -- be sure you have the backing to get your version and not a modified one passed).

Nonpolitical Family Advocacy

One way to counter the increasing self-centeredness and individualism of our culture is to promote more family activities in our communities. By this we mean activities which focus on the family itself, not the component parts of the family: picnics in which the entire extended family joins together, family reunions, adult/child sporting events and activities, community theatrical events such as historical pageants, parades, and so on.

The goal is to bring families together, *as families*, for wholesome fun and interaction, as opposed to separating them into age or interest-specific subgroups. "Family" events with alcohol are harmful in this regard, since adults and children are separated, psychologically if not always physically, by an activity that they cannot share. Activities which include sexual themes or innuendo are similarly divisive. Too often these days, so-called family events are anything but family oriented -- the phrase is more often used as a marketing ploy for selling products to parents of small children. Parents can have a very positive effect in the community by pointing out the difference between "family-centered" and "family-exploitative" events and supporting only the former.

RECOVERY FROM HOMOSEXUALITY

"I have...had occasion to review the results of psychotherapy with homosexuals, and been surprised by the findings. It is paradoxical that even though the politically active homosexual group denies the possibility of change, all studies from Schrench-Notzing on have found positive effects, virtually regardless of the kind of treatment used...Whether with hypnosis...psychoanalysis of any variety, educative psychotherapy, behavior therapy, and/or simple educational procedures, a considerable percentage of overt homosexuals became heterosexual...if the patients are motivated, whatever procedure is adopted...In this connection, public information is of the greatest importance. The misinformation spread by certain circles that 'homosexuality is untreatable by psychotherapy' does incalculable harm to thousands of men and women."

Dr. Reuben Fine, Director of New York Center for Psychiatric Training, "Psychoanalytic Theory," in *Male and Female Homosexuality: Psychological Approaches*, pp. 84-86, 1987.

"Some people believe that compassion for homosexuals means approving of their lifestyle, but I thank God that other people still have the guts to insist that it's wrong; otherwise I might still be trapped."

Richard "Jonah" Weller, Handbill, "The Voice They Want Silenced: A former homosexual man speaks out about homosexuality and the politics of dishonesty," 1992.

Be Active In Your Community

Participation in Ex-"Gay" Recovery Efforts

A growing number of cities and towns in America are hosting organizations which are dedicated to helping homosexuals to recover. Many of these efforts deserve much greater community support than they currently receive. As one might imagine, such organizations face vigorous opposition from local "gay" activists, who don't want to believe (and especially don't want anyone *else* to believe) that recovery from homosexual behavior is possible. At the same time, prospective supporters in the community may not even know of the existence of the group, since its members may be reluctant to advertise that they are in recovery from homosexuality. Recovering homosexuals benefit greatly from the friendship and companionship of confidently heterosexual same-sex mentors and friends. Finding your local group might take some effort, such as calling around to local churches, but such effort could prove very valuable to the community (and to recovering homosexuals, themselves). Every successfully recovered ex-"gay" is a walking, talking refutation of the lie that homosexuals can't change. (More information about the ex-"gay" movement is provided in the Epilogue).

No friend of parents, Parents and Friends of Lesbians and Gays (PFLAG) is an arm of the political "gay" movement which denies hope of recovery.

"Announcements like this that our kids have suddenly decided they're gay amount to a kind of murder of the family. Parents can't imagine things that are worse. It's something like a premature Alzheimer's disease; there's no more real communication, no more sharing of experience, now, or ever. Some great parents can say that this is okay. But, deep down, they know they are deluding themselves. This can mean the end of hopes and dreams for their kids -- that they will some day experience the extreme joys that have been repeated over and over again since civilization began, that they will become parents. And make them grandparents. To know that this isn't going to happen -- well, it's a sadness."

Charles W. Socarides, M.D. Homosexuality- A Freedom Too Far. pp. 281-282. 1995.

Epilogue

What To Do When
It's "Too Late"

In the words of a popular song from the '70s, "We don't know what we've got till it's gone." It's a sad fact that many of us take the best things in life for granted and only begin to appreciate them after they're gone. This is increasingly true for parents today, as more and more children are being recruited into the "gay" lifestyle. All of a parent's hopes and dreams for his child are suddenly darkened when he gets the bad news. It is likely that many of our readers are parents whose child has already "come out" to them as "gay." Others know or suspect that their child is involved in one or more homosexual relationships. In either case, it's too late to "recruit-proof" the child. But it's *never* too late for a child to recover his innate heterosexual orientation. However, as is so often true of things that we let "get out of hand," addressing this problem will take much more work than taking preventive action would have. Helping your "prodigal" son or daughter to recover from homosexuality will require more love, more patience, more understanding, and more humility from you than you may have ever given in the past. It will also require an honest *desire* to change on the part of your child. Sadly, this combination of parent and child commitment to recovery is rare.

BYPASSING PARENTS

"Don't raise the issue unless you're able to respond with confidence to the question, 'Are your sure?' Confusion on your part will increase your parents' confusion and decrease their confidence in your judgment."

READ · THIS · BEFORE
COMING OUT
TO YOUR PARENTS

"If you're wrestling with guilt or periods of depression, you'll be better off waiting to tell your parents."

"If you suspect they are capable of withdrawing college finances or forcing you out of the house, you may choose to wait until they do not have this weapon to hold over you."

"True Acceptance. Some parents get this far. Parents at this stage face up to their own guilt, that they are part of a guilty society, a homophobic society....This coming to terms with themselves may lead them to view the oppression of all gays and lesbians in a new light. They begin to speak out against the oppression....In short, they become committed to a cause."

Read This Before Coming Out To Your Parents, PFLAG brochure.

The Spider's Web

Typically, families of children who are recruited into homosexuality have poor parent/child communication. Thus, many children who experience gender identity confusion or feelings of sexual desire for persons of the same sex don't approach their parents during the early and most treatable stages of these problems. Instead, they go to someone else, a school counselor, a parent of a friend, an older friend or relative -- someone who appears more available and sympathetic to these types of problems. Unfortunately, these "sympathetic souls" are often people who have "bought in" to sexual orientation theory; some of them will be homosexuals themselves. Indeed, most of the organizations dedicated to "helping" children with questions about homosexuality (such as Parents and Friends of Lesbians and Gays -- PFLAG) are, quite literally, arms of the "gay" movement itself. Activists in these organizations are trained to discourage kids from approaching their parents *until their "gay" identity is firmly established.* Instead of getting help to overcome their problem, "gay"-vulnerable children become ensnared in the web of the "gay" community and parents only learn of the problem after their child has been fully assimilated into the homosexual subculture.

Closing the Sale

Notice that in this analysis we have not mentioned the physical homosexual seduction of children. We have described the more dangerous and insidious form of "gay" recruitment which attempts to indoctrinate the minds of the children themselves. Remember that in Step One we defined "gay" recruitment as the process of shaping opinions and attitudes about the "gay" lifestyle in such a way that a person is made more likely to initiate or respond positively to homosexual overtures. We also showed how, using sexual orientation theory, "gay" activists cause every child who comes under their influence to question whether he or she might be "gay." Throughout this book we have showed how "gay"

RUNNING UP THE WHITE PFLAG
RESIGNATION, NOT RECOVERY

"The well-known national organization 'Parents and Friends of Lesbians and Gays' (P-FLAG) serves as a support group for parents seeking guidance for their homosexual children. P-FLAG is recommended as a resource group by the U.S. Department of Education and U.S. Department of Justice in its upcoming manual, 'Preventing Youth Hate Crime.' Many schools, community agencies, and even nationally syndicated newspaper columnists refer families to it. P-FLAG has affiliates in all 50 states, with about 70,000 families among its membership.

A look at some of P-FLAG's literature and recommended books, however, reveals an approach to child guidance which is consistently both *sexually* and *socially* radical....Some of the recommended books are relatively 'tame' on the surface, justifying teenaged homosexual experimentation with the usual 'This is me. This is who I am.' Others go much further-glorifying sex with animals, witchcraft, feminist goddess worship, worship of sexual pleasure as a form of religion, promiscuity with hundreds of partners, bisexual orgies, and voyeurism..."

"Recommended Reading for Teenagers? A Closer Look at P-FLAG," *Narth Bulletin*. pp. 1,16, April 1998.

propaganda misleads the public, especially young people, about homosexuality, the "gay" movement and its opponents. Finally, in this chapter, we see the endgame -- what is called, in sales, the "close." The young person, bombarded from early childhood with the messages that "gay" is good, that he himself might be "gay," and that opponents of the "gay" movement (including his parents) are "homophobic" and untrustworthy, voluntarily presents himself at the door of the "gay" community, looking for answers to his troubling questions. Inside, with smiles of understanding and acceptance await experienced "gay" recruiters who themselves once stood at that same door. "Come in," they beckon warmly, "We've been waiting for you. You're finally home."

Respond Lovingly

We offer the following advice from Mark Pertuit of Desert Stream Ministries:

> When it's "too late": It's not! Change is possible. The personality is more fluid than many would otherwise believe. [Parents] with a child who has homosexual issues should...bend over backwards to avoid critical relating and shaming. They should affirm the child as a person in the image of God, but should not in any way identify the child as a homosexual. The child is not a homosexual. To take on that identity is to lose a big battle...[O]ffer the notion that healing is possible [without pushing too hard]...pushing them only makes them push back, or seek [counseling] for the wrong reasons.

Discourage "Coming Out"

To the uninitiated, "coming out" is simply a term for announcing to others that one is "gay." In reality, "coming out" is a multi-purpose tactic for advancing the "gay" agenda -- part psychological conditioning (of the new recruit), part political grandstanding. Rather than being a single event, "coming out"

AVERTING FURTHER HARM

"For years it never occurred to me to define myself as a homosexual. The course I followed was wrong and destructive; others besides myself were hurt by it. But if someone had come along when I was fourteen or fifteen and forced me to declare myself a homosexual, how much more tragedy would have occurred. I thank God I was not exposed to this."

Alan Medinger, "Adolescents and Homosexuality - Close Look at a Major Study," pp. 1-2. Regeneration News. February, 1993.

"Don't accept the currently fashionable cop out that it isn't a problem. Try to talk to your kid. Listen to him. Don't attack, don't get hysterical, don't engage in threats. (Don't be too hard on yourself. It may help to realize that there are some terrible parents who don't have this problem, and some great parents who do.) Wait for a calm moment and then explain to him that you're worried about whatever you've noticed concerning his behavior or his choice of friends. Tell him about your values, and why you're dead set against same-sex sex. He's still your kid, your young adult. And he needs your support. You're not going to stop loving him, or ignore him, much less banish him from your home. That will tell him a lot about you and your love for him. That alone -- the sense of being loved no matter what -- does wonders. Same thing goes for your daughter. Your kids need your help."

Charles W. Socarides, M.D. Homosexuality- A Freedom Too Far. pp. 277-280. 1995.

involves a *process* which begins with "gay"-affirming counseling (which activists describe as "coming out" to oneself) and culminates with a declaration to the world. Assimilation into the "gay" community through homosexual relationships and political activities makes up the greater part of the "coming out" process for most fledgling "gays." The "coming out" process is used by the "gay" movement to ensure the psychological commitment of its members. Any public declaration has this effect (consider how difficult it is for couples to break off an engagement to be married after they have announced it publicly), but an announcement that one is homosexual virtually "locks the door and throws away the key" to the possibility of changing one's mind. Other declarations can be recanted, and will have minimal lasting effect, but declaring oneself "gay" means branding oneself with a stigma that is all but impossible to erase.

For this reason, parents should strongly discourage a child from making a public declaration of his "gay" self-label. Parents can often prevent such a declaration because "coming out" to parents is usually a preliminary stage to going public. If a public announcement seems imminent you might approach the issue by asking the child to delay the announcement until after he or she has had the chance to talk with an experienced recovery counselor or an ex-homosexual.

Don't Be Manipulated

A common emotional response shared by parents of self-identified "gays" is guilt. The "gay" movement is poised to exploit this emotion as part of the process of guiding a new recruit through the process of "coming out" to you. PFLAG was created for this purpose. The PFLAG strategy is to use emotional blackmail and coercion to transform every parent of a self-identified "gay" into a spokesperson for the "gay" cause. The message given is that if you *really* loved your child, you would accept his or her *lifestyle* (not just accept him or her as a person). Typically, a parent is accused of being ignorant and "homophobic" if he or she does not embrace the

"What I am saying is that being gay is an acquired identity....Since homosexuality is an acquired identity, it makes sense that you can choose to change that identity....'Once gay, always gay?' That is what I used to think. Not anymore."

Jeff Conrad, *You Don't Have To Be Gay*, p.11, 1992.

child's homosexual choice. *No* opposition to homosexuality is deemed acceptable: only full acceptance of the homosexual lifestyle itself is applauded.

Your best response to the PFLAG tactic is to reject *it* but not your child. Love the child, but don't condone the lifestyle. In sorting through these issues, you can take advantage of an organization called Parents and Friends of Ex-Gays (PFOX). In terms of offering hope for recovery, PFLAG says "tough luck," but PFOX offers genuine "tough *love*" and the chance of heterosexual normalcy and emotional health for your child.

Never Give Up Hope

As the parent of a self-identified "gay," a parent who desires recovery for his child, you should know that several factors can work in your favor. First, sexual orientation is not immutable; people can and do change their sexual identity every day. Second, the "gay" lifestyle is not gay, but miserable. We believe that every homosexual eventually wants out. Try to be there with encouraging words when that happens. Third, the ex-"gay" movement is growing stronger every day. In time, it may be able to reach your child through its own network of recovered homosexuals.

Try to imagine your child as he was when he was first learning to walk, or ride a bike, or to multiply fractions. He needed your strength, sympathy, patience and love then, and he needs it today even more. Never accept his comfort with his disorder as the final word. Always offer hope for change; always have unconditional love for the person caught in the "gay" lifestyle.

RECOMMENDED RESOURCES

General Pro-Family

American Family Association
PO Drawer 2440
Tupelo, MS 38803
601-844-5036

Americans For Truth About Homosexuality
Lambda Report
PO Box 45252
Washington, D.C. 20026-5252
703-491-7975

Family Research Council
801 G St. NW
Washington, DC 20001
202-393-2100

Family Research Institute
PO Box 62640
Colorado Springs, CO 80962
303-681-3113

Focus on the Family
PO Box 35500
Colorado Springs, CO 80935-3550

Stop Promoting Homosexuality International
PO Box 27843
Honolulu, HI 96827
808-523-7739

Traditional Values Coalition
PO Box 940
Anaheim, CA 92815

Ex-"Gay" and "Gay" Recovery

National Association for Research and Therapy of Homosexuality (NARTH)
16633 Ventura Blvd, Suite 1340
Encino, CA 91436
818-789-4440

Parents and Friends of Ex-Gays (PFOX)
1017 12th Street NW
Washington, D.C. 20005
202-371-0800

Exodus International (international network of ex-"gay" groups)
PO Box 77652
Seattle, WA 98177
206-784-7799

Regeneration Books (Clearinghouse)
PO Box 9830
Baltimore, MD 21284-9830
410-661-4337

Sex Ed

National Abstinence Clearing House
801 E. 41st Street
Sioux Falls, SD 57105
605-335-3643

Homeschooling

National Home Education Research Institute
PO Box 13939
Salem, OR 97309
503-364-1490

WARNING SIGNS

of a teenager who may be seduced into homosexuality.

The following information for parents is provided by former homosexual, Jerry Armelli, M.Ed.. Reprinted from *Reaching Out* newsletter, April 1998.

Isolation from family and/or friends. This could include the son or daughter leaving friends they once "hung out" with to "hang out" with a new set of "friends."

The teen does not "fit in" to society's mold of masculine/feminine. In some instances when a child does not fit into the traditional gender role insecurities about one's gender identity may be challenged with thoughts like: "Why don't I like the same things that other boys/girls do?" "I'm supposed to do that....Why doesn't that interest me?" "I don't like the same things my brothers/sisters do...Why?"

Gender disassociation. The teen may overtly display a dislike or intimidation of traditional gender roles. This may be accompanied by the over-attaching of oneself to the opposite gender group. Avoiding one's own gender group may be a sign that the child is disassociating with the identity of his/her gender group.

Victim of molestation. Sexual assault, either witnessed or endured, can be very destructive to the development of a secure gender identity.

Obsession with "special friend." This is not to be confused with a healthy identification with peers that adolescents go through. This preoccupation with a "special friend" can be described as an unreasonable and persistent...feeling towards another.

Bitterness. Open rebellion. Certainly, this is a more obvious warning sign. Often times when parents come to [our meetings] for the first time they describe their son or daughter with the following words, "It is as though they are part of a cult...they have new friends, new language, new look...they are not the same person."

Absence of same-gender parent/significant other. Has there been a divorce, separation, death, sickness that has separated the child from the same-gender parent? Is the same-gender parent emotionally non-engaging?